# "It Is What It Is"

# "It Is What It Is"

## Saving AmericanWest Bank

### A Story of Leadership

By

Charles J Thayer

*Copyright@ 2010 by Charles J Thayer*

*All Rights Reserved*
*First Edition*

**Chartwell Capital Ltd**
**420 Isle of Capri**
**Fort Lauderdale, FL 33301**

*www.ChartwellCapital.com*

*ISBN: 978-1-4583-0002-7*

## Contents

| | | |
|---|---|---|
| Preface | | 7 |
| Dedication | | 9 |
| Acknowledgements | | 11 |
| Forward | | 13 |
| AmericanWest Profile | | 15 |
| Introduction | | 17 |
| Chapter 1 | It Started in Kentucky | 21 |
| Chapter 2 | Mountains of Georgia | 27 |
| Chapter 3 | Coast of California | 29 |
| Chapter 4 | Welcome to Spokane | 33 |
| Chapter 5 | Interim Chief Executive | 43 |
| Chapter 6 | Financial Meltdown | 57 |
| Chapter 7 | Government Response | 61 |
| Chapter 8 | Big Hat – No Cattle | 69 |
| Chapter 9 | Groundhog Day | 75 |
| Chapter 10 | Dead End Detour | 87 |
| Chapter 11 | Question of Bankruptcy | 93 |
| Chapter 12 | Tone at the Top | 111 |
| Chapter 13 | Regulatory Policy | 113 |
| The Board of Directors | | 125 |
| The Senior Management Team | | 127 |
| The Asset/Liability Committee | | 129 |
| The Attorneys | | 131 |
| The Author | | 133 |
| Abbreviations & Definitions | | 135 |
| Tombstone | | 137 |

## *Preface*

The Board of Directors is grateful to Charles for sharing the story of AmericanWest and the fine individuals who guided it through significant challenges in market conditions, financial obstacles, and personnel changes.

In June of 2008, the Board made the decision to terminate our relationship with our existing CEO and Pat Rusnak was appointed interim CEO. Pat demonstrated practical, hands on experience and led the management team with proven authority and a tested track record. He immediately began the task of actively searching for needed capital.

Pat worked very well with our Board and working together we faced obstacles not seen since the Great Depression. We performed complimentary roles, ensuring that our whole performance was greater than the sum of our parts. Together, Pat and the Board determined strategy in an ever-changing environment.

In conclusion, I am obviously saddened by the loss to our shareholders. On the other hand, I am proud that the sale of the Bank was accomplished without government intervention or taxpayer support. Our customers will be positively impacted, employees given new opportunities, and branches in small markets left intact.

On behalf of our Board, THANK YOU!

Craig D. Eerkes
Chairman of the Board
AmericanWest Bank
December 16, 2010

## *Dedication*

This book is dedicated to Pat Rusnak and his family. I hope the book provides his family with a view of Pat's long workdays over the past three years and helps them better understand what a remarkable feat he and his entire management team at AmericanWest accomplished.

Photo: AWBC
Patrick J. Rusnak

It is also impossible to ignore the dedication that the Board of Directors and all of the employees of AmericanWest Bank exhibited during the period described in this book. The eventual success of the Bank's recapitalization would not have been possible without the day-to-day commitment of the Bank's employees to serving the Bank's customers – the ultimate value of the Bank was based on their customer relationships.

## Acknowledgements

In the beginning I just wanted to write a short story describing the successful recapitalization of AmericanWest Bank. A little something I could share with the Bank's management team – without their efforts there would be no story to tell. This book started out as a small project that took on a life of its own.

The book could not have been completed without the help of what Humphrey Bogart described in Casablanca as the "Usual Suspects" – which in this case includes my wife Molly, who tolerated my project as it grew and proofread multiple versions.

Special thanks must also go to Linda Williams and Jay Simmons at AmericanWest. Although I drafted the original versions of numerous documents submitted to both the Board of Directors and AmericanWest's regulators, I must admit the final versions of these documents were greatly enhanced by Linda's and Jay's editing skills. A rough draft of this book was also provided both to Linda and Jay for review prior to its publication and once again I am the beneficiary of their knowledge and editorial skill.

I also had the privilege of watching Jay guide the legal process for the Bank's final recapitalization plan from my initial memo to a successful result. I became a spectator to events – concepts are worthless without professional execution. Jay's contribution was essential to saving AmericanWest from seizure by the FDIC.

Finally, this book would not be possible without the technology that permitted an amateur author like myself to "self publish". The reader is warned not to expect a literary masterpiece. The opinions expressed and all the errors are mine alone.

# Forward

2008: AmericanWest Bancorporation (AWBC) and its subsidiary bank, AmericanWest Bank, were in trouble, serious trouble, but the AmericanWest Board of Directors and management team were committed to saving the Bank and avoiding its seizure by the Federal Deposit Insurance Corporation. This is their story.

This is a story of executive leadership during one of the most stressful periods of our nation's financial history. This is not a "how to" book, it's simply a story of the exceptional leadership skills exhibited by the entire management team at AmericanWest as they faced and conquered the unforgiving challenges presented by the economic events of the past three years.

In many respects it's not fair to single out one individual when the Bank's successful recapitalization was due to many people – a true team effort. But even great teams need a leader and AmericanWest was very fortunate to have Pat Rusnak.

I decided to publish this book because I believe it's important to share a community bank's success story at a time when too many "bankers" are considered to be the "enemy" by the press and public.

Small regional banks like AmericanWest were largely neglected by our leaders in Washington, D.C., while the government acted to "bail out" many of the nation's "too large to fail" financial institutions (whether they needed it or not) following the bankruptcy of Lehman Brothers and the financial meltdown that occurred in September 2008.

This is the story of how one small regional bank that government officials considered "small enough to fail' managed to save itself.

## *AmericanWest*

AmericanWest Bancorporation is a $1.5 billion bank holding company based in Spokane, Washington.

Its principal operating subsidiary, AmericanWest Bank, operates a total of 56 financial centers.

In most cases the distinction between AmericanWest Bancorporation, the bank holding company that owns the Bank, and the subsidiary Bank is not very important. In the case of AmericanWest this difference became the most important element in its final recapitalization.

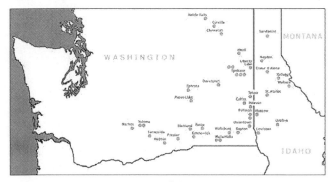

Maps courtesy of AmericanWest

Founded in 1974, the Bank operates 38 financial centers in Washington and Idaho and 18 financial centers in Utah under the name Far West Bank.

The unwavering dedication and extensive knowledge of more than 500 employees was an essential contribution to saving AmericanWest Bank.

# Introduction

*"Charles, this is Pat, I would like you to fly to Spokane."*

That's how this chapter of my relationship with Pat Rusnak began. My firm, Chartwell Capital, was retained as a financial advisor to AmericanWest in August 2008 and served in that capacity through December 2010. This relationship provided the opportunity to work with Rusnak and his management team throughout this challenging period in financial history.

You will be disappointed if you expect an exposé, as no confidential information or secrets are disclosed. The majority of the financial information contained in the following pages was obtained from the Company's press releases, public filings with the Securities & Exchange Commission, court documents or public reports filed with bank regulators. The few exceptions are related to the Bank's remarkable liquidity story and are included with permission of AmericanWest.

The idea behind the book was to write a story that could be shared with the Bank's management team in recognition of their remarkable achievement. The book describes how the Board of Directors, Rusnak, the management team and the employees of AmericanWest managed to navigate their way through the financial hurricane of 2008 and save their Bank.

Note: Throughout this book "Company" refers to AmericanWest Bancorporation, the holding company, and "Bank" refers to the subsidiary, AmericanWest Bank. AWBC is the NASDAQ stock-trading symbol for AmericanWest Bancorporation.

That phone call to me in August 2008 was the beginning of this chapter with Pat Rusnak, but it's not the beginning of the story.

Our story starts in 1998 at Trans Financial Bank in Kentucky and includes stops along the way in the mountains of Georgia and along the northern coast of California.

Having the opportunity to work with Pat from time to time during his banking career has provided me with a unique perspective on Pat's character and his no-nonsense approach to management. I have witnessed bank employees deliver bad news to Pat in numerous meetings over the years, and this book's title is based on Pat's constructive approach to bad news. I have never witnessed Pat "shooting the messenger" and as a result people keep him informed. He accepts the message ("It Is What It Is") and immediately starts to focus on the next steps.

I hope this book provides a few leadership lessons, but most of all it's about the combined effort of the people at AmericanWest to solve problems and save their Bank.

*Charles J Thayer*
Fort Lauderdale
December 2010

*"It Is What It Is"*

## Chapter One

## It Started in Kentucky

Our story starts in Kentucky at Trans Financial Bank in Bowling Green. Many bankers of Rusnak's generation enjoyed smooth sailing during the late 1990s. Rusnak missed that boat – he didn't join the crew of a bank that enjoyed an easy voyage based on the rising economic tide. His early involvement in navigating the financial storm at Trans Financial helped to prepare him for storms to come and the financial hurricane of 2008.

In 1996, Trans Financial was a $2.0 billion multi-bank holding company based in the south central Kentucky community of Bowling Green, home of the Corvette plant. Trans Financial had grown rapidly, more than doubling it size through a series of community bank acquisitions in the early 1990s. In 1993 Trans Financial's CEO initiated a strategic decision to change this community banking organization into a diversified financial services provider.

The result three years later was a company burdened with a wide array of poorly performing nonbank operations. Three years of disappointing results culminated in action by its board of directors to replace the company's chief executive officer (CEO).

Vince Berta, the company's Chief Financial Officer (CFO), was promoted to President & CEO in June 1996. Berta had joined Trans Financial as CFO from PNC Bank a few years earlier. Berta quickly shifted Trans Financial's focus back to its core banking franchise and the company exited its non-core businesses.

Management also addressed credit quality issues and increased loan loss reserves. I believe Berta's experience at Trans Financial made him a great early role model for Rusnak – Berta not only knew how to analyze a problem, he had the experience and management skill to execute the solution.

Berta began his banking career in the early 1980's at Citizens Fidelity Bank in Louisville, Kentucky, where I was CFO at the time. An unlikely candidate, Berta had no banking experience when my Senior Vice President of Finance hired him as a financial analyst. Her judgment was superb and he quickly became the "go to" person for any complex problem.

Berta and I both benefited from working with David Grissom, the bank's Chairman and CEO. As a young attorney, Grissom joined two of his law partners to found what is now Humana. Already a very successful attorney and businessman, he joined Citizens Fidelity as Vice Chairman in 1973 at the age of 34. I won't recount the financial turmoil of the late 1970's and early 1980's, but it proved to be a great environment to develop financial management skills.

Under Grissom's leadership, Citizens Fidelity successfully navigated the impact of two oil shocks, 20% interest rates and 10% unemployment. As CEO Grissom was instrumental in introducing the legislation that permitted multi-state expansion for Kentucky banks, and Citizens Fidelity grew from a $1 billion Louisville-based bank to a highly profitable $5 billion organization (1996 return on equity was 19%) with offices in Kentucky, Indiana and Ohio.

PNC acquired Citizens Fidelity in 1986 and following several other acquisitions PNC became the 12th largest banking group in the nation by 1989 with over $40 billion in assets. I had moved to PNC headquarters in Pittsburgh following the acquisition of Citizens Fidelity and for several years, served as Executive Vice President – Finance of PNC.

Berta succeeded me as CFO of Citizens Fidelity following PNC's acquisition of the bank. His career eventually took him to PNC's headquarters in Pittsburgh.

In 1993 Berta was enticed by an offer to become CFO of Trans Financial and moved to Bowling Green.

Meanwhile, Rusnak started his banking career with a community bank in Pennsylvania following his 1985 graduation from Saint Joseph's University in Philadelphia. Rusnak joined Trans Financial in 1995 as Senior Assistant Controller in the finance division working for Berta.

Following Berta's elevation to CEO, Rusnak's financial responsibilities were expanded to include management oversight of the internal loan review department and he became a member of Trans Financial's special assets committee. Little did Rusnak know how important this early credit experience would be to his future banking career.

Working with Berta, Rusnak was a member of a select group of executives who developed and implemented Berta's new business plan. It's important to recognize that Berta's plan was a combination of core banking growth, divesting noncore businesses and improving operating efficiency – building a business, not just a cost cutting exercise.

Trans Financial's management team also included a young lawyer named Jay Simmons. As told later in our story, Simmons and Rusnak were destined to cross paths again at AmericanWest.

Trans Financial served as the opening round of Rusnak's professional experience where he had the opportunity to contribute to strategic decisions that resulted in significant financial success. He gained valuable experience by undertaking strategic reviews of selected bank operations and helping to implement plans for corrective action. This early experience was good preparation for the financial and operational challenges Rusnak would later face at other institutions.

The following table clearly illustrates how execution of the 1996 plan produced significant results in 1997:

**Trans Financial**

| $ millions | 1995 | 1996 | 1997 |
|---|---|---|---|
| Total Assets | $1,795 | $2,003 | $2,113 |
| Return on Equity | 12.6% | 5.3% | 17.0% |
| Efficiency Ratio | 72% | 72% | 61% |
| Loan Losses | .17% | .86% | .38% |

The Trans Financial chapter ends with one of the highest acquisition premiums reported in the 1990's. The company's improved financial performance attracted the interest of several potential aquirors in 1998. In response, Berta undertook an analysis of Trans Financial's strategic alternatives and sought advice from selected legal and investment firms, including my firm, Chartwell Capital.

Berta had extensive merger and acquisition experience and knew how to manage the evaluation of Trans Financial's strategic alternatives. He was my key resource as Citizens Fidelity acquired 10 banks in the 1980's and was at my side during our negotiations to be acquired by PNC. His analysis indicated that the best value for Trans Financial's shareholders would be the acquisition by a high quality institution.

Berta sought the best advice available and engaged Ed Herlihy at Wachtell Lipton in New York to provide both legal and strategic advice. The result was a transaction with Star Bank (now US Bank) at 4.6 times tangible book value.

# # #

Rusnak played an important supporting role in the Star Bank transaction, and he clearly learned the significance of seeking the best advice available from people like Herlihy, as well as the important criteria required for successful bank mergers. These skills were quickly tested after he moved to Georgia.

## Chapter Two

## Mountains of Georgia

Star Bank missed an opportunity when they overlooked a young "assistant" Controller following their acquisition of Trans Financial. Rusnak quickly landed a position in 1998 as Controller of United Community Banks, Inc. and his family moved to Blairsville, Georgia.

This will be a short but important chapter. It marks Rusnak's first move into a senior management role. At United Community, a $1.8 billion institution, he was actively involved in the acquisition and integration of four banks and one technology consulting company.

He gained first hand experience with investors, investment bankers and the capital markets, and he developed a new capital plan that ultimately led to a $30 million rights offering and a $40 million trust preferred offering.

*"Charles, this is Pat Rusnak.*

*Vince Berta suggested I give you a call."*

That call was my introduction to Rusnak at United Community Banks. Rusnak had recognized the benefits of consolidating United Community's multi-state banking operations into a more cohesive business model. However, United Community's historic acquisition strategy had been based on maintaining local charters and local management autonomy.

Jimmy Tallent, United Community's CEO, was willing to consider a strategic change but he required a thoughtful plan that he believed could be executed without disrupting the company's successful business model.

I still remember the offsite meeting where Tallent challenged every aspect of the plan Rusnak and I presented. However, Rusnak's recommendations were accepted and successfully implemented. United Community restructured its business model by consolidating operations and centralizing credit and banking services for the company's two state area.

The benefit to United Community's financial performance was evident with the year 2000 results as illustrated below:

## United Community Banks

| $ million | 1998 | 1999 | 2000 |
|---|---|---|---|
| Total Assets | $ 1,813 | $2,384 | $2,528 |
| Return on Equity | 14.8% | 14.7% | 15.9% |
| Efficiency Ratio | 68% | 68% | 65% |

United Community was viewed as a well managed, high performance institution. Rusnak was a likely target for an executive search, because future promotion appeared to be blocked as United Community's CFO was only a few years older than Rusnak. As a result, Rusnak responded when sought out in 2000 and was recruited to be Chief Financial Officer of Humboldt Bancorp in Eureka, California.

## Chapter Three

## *Coast of California*

Rusnak accepted the CFO position at Humboldt Bancorp in 2000 and the family moved to Eureka on the northern coast of California.

As Executive Vice President and Chief Financial Officer he was responsible for all finance, accounting and strategic planning functions for this $800 million bank holding company. Rusnak quickly put his prior experience to work.

In 2001, Rusnak initiated a strategic review to evaluate Humboldt's existing lines of business, potential acquisition opportunities and potential merger partners. The company's CEO announced his intention to retire shortly after Rusnak arrived and the fundamental objective of Rusnak's analysis was to evaluate the potential value of "build" versus "sell".

*"Charles, this is Pat."*

It's always been Rusnak's practice to call me early in the morning – prior to 8 A.M. Eastern Time. I leave it to your imagination about the impact of time zones.

I was pleased that Rusnak invited me to assist with the 2001 evaluation of Humboldt's operations, and we included investment bankers from Keefe Bruyette & Woods in the process to evaluate both the potential for acquisitions by Humboldt and Humboldt's acquisition by potential merger partners.

Following careful analysis of the build versus sell alternatives and extensive discussions, the board elected to remain independent and recruit a new CEO following the retirement of the current CEO.

Robert Daugherty was recruited from Zions Bank in April 2002 and Daugherty and Rusnak began executing the strategy developed in 2001 by Rusnak.

**Humboldt Bancorp**

| $ million | 2000 | 2001 | 2002 | 2003 | 2004 |
|---|---|---|---|---|---|
| Assets | $852 | $957 | $1,031 | $1,044 | $1,456 |
| Return on Equity | 14.2% | 8.6% | 13.8% | 11.3% | (a) |
| Efficiency Ratio | 72% | 75% | 72% | 72% | 71% |
| Loan Losses | .33% | .24% | .21% | .12% | .06% |

(a) Humboldt was acquired by Umpqua in 2004

As illustrated above, a key component of the plan was designed to reduce credit risk. Our analysis resulted in the immediate liquidation of the company's leasing subsidiary in 2001. The situation at the leasing subsidiary could only be described as a "financial and operating mess." Liquidation of the subsidiary was a complex matter and required expert legal advice. Rusnak retained the services of Henry Fields, an attorney at Morrison & Foerster, to provide guidance as Rusnak liquidated the subsidiary's non-performing assets and negotiated the sale of the subsidiary's high-risk retained securitization assets.

Rusnak's analysis also included an evaluation of the credit risks and rewards associated with Humboldt's Merchant Bankcard Services. The evaluation concluded that Humboldt's overall risk profile would be enhanced by the strategic sale of its Merchant Bankcard Services and refocusing efforts on community banking. Rusnak successfully negotiated the sale of Merchant Bankcard Services in 2002.

In addition, the plan included the sale of selected branch locations and the relocation of corporate headquarters to Sacramento. Humboldt's core markets, combined with the acquisition of California Independent Bancorp, contributed to the growth of Humboldt Bank from $800 million to $1.4 billion. This growth also required the successful conversion to a new core processing system to support Humboldt's expansion.

The divesture of leasing and bankcard merchant processing lowered Humboldt's risk profile and credit quality steadily improved.

Umpqua Holdings, a $5 billion bank holding company based in Portland, Oregon, acquired Humboldt Bancorp in March 2004. This acquisition of Humboldt and its 27 locations was Umpqua's initial entry into California. Following the acquisition, Rusnak was asked to join Umpqua as EVP & CFO of the California Region.

Meanwhile, Daugherty moved to Spokane as the new President & Chief Executive Officer of AmericanWest Bancorporation and its subsidiary, AmericanWest Bank. Daugherty and Rusnak would link up again in Spokane at a later date.

Rusnak remained in Sacramento and served as a member of Umpqua's executive management group. He played a key role in the merger integration process and the initial corporate-wide implementation of Sarbanes-Oxley Section 404 compliance. With respect to Section 404, he developed a new allowance for loan losses methodology and impaired loan policy.

Western Sierra Bancorp, also located in the Sacramento area, initiated a search for a Chief Operating Officer in 2005 and, not surprisingly, identified an ideal candidate in their backyard. Rusnak was recruited to Western Sierra where he was responsible for management of finance/accounting, compliance, internal audit, human resources, operations and information technology functions of this $1.3 billion multi-bank holding company.

Rusnak served as Western Sierra's principal liaison with bank regulators, and successfully negotiated the termination of a merger with a bank that had significant risks that had not been identified in the original due diligence process.

Western Sierra Bancorp was acquired by Umpqua Holdings Corporation in 2006, providing Daugherty an opportunity to recruit Rusnak to Spokane.

# Chapter Four

# Welcome to Spokane

September 2006 (AWBC Stock $22.00): Rusnak probably didn't appreciate it at the time, but he was well prepared for his move to Spokane as Chief Operating Officer of AmericanWest in September, following a few months of relaxation and reflection. He had 10 years experience in managing problems, divesting businesses, and improving operating efficiency combined with successful internal growth and growth by acquisition.

Few community bank finance and operating executives had the credit experience Rusnak had gained during the nation's 10-year boom economy that had concealed a growing mountain of real estate debt that would soon turn ugly. His experience would soon be put to the test.

When Daugherty joined AmericanWest two years earlier in September 2004, it was a $1.0 billion bank holding company headquartered in Spokane with operations in Washington and Idaho. Upon arrival he successfully addressed potential loan problems and announced the termination of a Supervisory Directive that had been issued based upon the Bank's operations under prior management.

In the press release announcing the termination of the Supervisory Directive Daugherty stated:

*"There are no regulatory restrictions on our growth, other than those generally applicable to the banking industry as a whole, now that the bank is no longer restricted by this supervisory enforcement action. Coupling this with the recent lifting of the memorandum of understanding to which we also were subject over the past year, we are now poised to move forward,*

confident of our ability to grow during 2006 both organically and through expansion."

Prior to joining Humboldt Bancorp in 2002, Daugherty had run Draper Bank in Utah and later worked at Zions Bank in Salt Lake City for a year after it acquired Draper Bank. He was very familiar with the Utah banking market and still maintained a residence in the Salt Lake area. For Daugherty, it was the natural arena for future expansion once AmericanWest had retuned to solid footing.

By mid 2006 Daugherty had grown the Bank to $1.4 billion with a combination of internal growth and the 2006 acquisition of Columbia Trust Bank in Washington. AmericanWest began its expansion into Utah with the opening of a Salt Lake-based loan production office in the Spring of 2006. This new loan production office focused principally on the origination of large residential development and multi-family construction loans, and quickly put together a sizable portfolio of loans.

Rusnak joined Daugherty as Executive Vice President & Chief Operating Officer at AmericanWest, with responsibility for executive management of finance/accounting, legal, compliance, internal audit, facilities, information technology, operations, human resources and residential mortgage banking functions.

Just prior to Rusnak's arrival in Spokane in late September, Daugherty had negotiated the acquisition of Far West Bank, a $400 million bank based in Provo, Utah, which had not yet been announced. Rusnak believed he was joining an experienced CEO at a bank with a sound strategy for future growth.

April 2007 (AWBC Stock $21.00): AmericanWest received shareholder and regulatory approval for the acquisition of Far West, and the Bank's Salt Lake loan production office was consolidated into Far West when the transaction was completed. The foothold in Utah was complete – the die was cast.

Upon joining the Bank in the fall of 2006, Rusnak had expressed concern to Daugherty about the financing structure of the Bank's acquisitions - the cash payout in the Far West merger required the issuance of an additional $20 million of Trust Preferred Securities (TruPS), effectively doubling the holding company's TruPS borrowing to $40 million. This was in addition to $100 million of intangible assets (goodwill) related to the Columbia Trust and Far West acquisitions that was added to the balance sheet during 2006 and 2007.

Asset quality problems in Utah began to surface in late summer of 2007. The expansion into Utah was to become the "Achilles Heel" of AmericanWest.

No surprise that these problems were real estate-related, and action was initiated to address the problems being identified in the Utah portfolio. The Bank ceased origination of new residential development loans in August 2007 in recognition of the deteriorating market conditions. The bank also initiated a careful review of residential construction and development loans, resulting in a significant increase in the Bank's provision for loan losses for the fourth quarter of 2007.

When results were reported for 2007, loan losses had doubled over the prior year and the provision to the loan loss reserve had tripled.

January 31, 2008 (AWBC Stock $13.00): The Company reported a net loss of $3 million for the fourth quarter of 2007. The fourth quarter financial results were negatively impacted by a provision for loan losses of $15 million principally due to deterioration in the residential construction and development segment of the loan portfolio. For the year, the Company reported net income of $9 million.

Daugherty stated in the Company's earnings release in January 2008: *"Our fourth quarter operating results, although reflective of the difficult overall operating environment and continued deterioration of the residential real estate sector, were clearly a disappointment. We took a conservative approach with respect to downgrading and placing loans on non-accrual status, recognizing charge-offs and building the allowance to loan ratio by over 20 basis points during the fourth quarter, consistent with our credit risk management practices."*

In early 2008, Rusnak made the first move designed to allow improvement of AmericanWest's capital position by initiating a proposal for blank-check preferred stock at the Company level. It would soon be apparent that capital market conditions for all financial institutions were rapidly deteriorating as a result of sharply deteriorating mortgage credit.

March 14, 2008: Bear Stearns had been in the headlines for months and had been encountering liquidity problems following the collapse of two affiliated hedge funds in 2007. On this Friday, the Federal Reserve Bank of New York announced that it had agreed to provide a $25 billion loan to Bear Stearns to provide liquidity for up to 28 days.

March 16, 2008: Over that weekend, the Federal Reserve changed the terms and arranged for JP Morgan to purchase Bear Stearns for $2.00 per share. The announcement of the acquisition on Sunday night represented a staggering loss for Bear Stearns shareholders, as the shares had traded over $90 per share just a few weeks earlier in February and over $170 per share in early 2007. Confidence in the value of Wall Street firms was shattered and the Federal Reserve opened the Discount Window for the first time to other investment banks.

Ben Bernanke, Chairman of the Federal Reserve Board, defended the transaction by stating the bankruptcy of Bear Stearns would have caused a "chaotic unwinding" of investments across U.S. markets. His statement would prove very prophetic in September following the bankruptcy of Lehman Brothers.

The relationship between market confidence and liquidity for the highly leveraged Wall Street firms was being severely tested. Chairman Cox at the Securities and Exchange Commission observed that the collapse of Bear Stearns was due to a lack of confidence, not a lack of capital. Ultimately the market rumors about the firm became self-fulfilling.

The markets were near panic following reports that other Wall Street firms were being threatened by the continuing liquidity crisis. Investors largely ignored governmental and regulatory statements that the crisis was isolated and contained. Given the circumstances it was not the best time for a community bank like AmericanWest to enter the capital markets for fresh capital.

April 24, 2008 (AWBC Stock $7.00): The month following the near failure of Bear Stearns, the Company reported a net loss of $32 million. Included in the first quarter results was a non-cash goodwill impairment charge of $27 million. This goodwill impairment charge represented approximately 21% of the Company's total goodwill balance, the majority of which was recorded in connection with the acquisitions of Far West in April 2007 and Columbia Trust in March 2006. The impairment was principally due to the reduction in the Company's market capitalization since December 31, 2007, and declining bank merger and acquisition valuations for recent transactions.

Goodwill is excluded from regulatory capital; the charge (which was not deductible for income tax purposes) did not have any adverse impact on the regulatory capital ratios of the Company or the Bank. Both the Company and the Bank continued to exceed the federal regulatory standards for "well capitalized" as of March 31, 2008.

Although AmericanWest was still considered well capitalized, it became clear to management and the Board of Directors that additional capital would be required to address the Bank's financial problems. In addition, Rusnak coordinated management's detailed review of the performance of the Bank, and the Board would determine in early summer that a change in strategic direction was necessary.

The Company received approval for blank-check preferred stock at its annual shareholders meeting in April. And in order to preserve existing capital, the Board suspended the cash dividend on the Company's common stock that same month.

March 2008: The Board engaged the investment banking firm of Sandler O'Neill + Partners, L.P. to assist with an evaluation of strategic alternatives, including the issuance of trust preferred securities, private common and preferred equity, the divestiture of assets, and the sale of AmericanWest to another financial institution.

Al Glowasky, the Managing Director based in Sandler O'Neill's San Francisco office, accepted the challenge. Glowasky was to play a very important role for AmericanWest during the next two and one-half years, and the ultimate completion of the Bank's recapitalization is due in large part to his personal commitment and tireless efforts.

Working with Glowasky, the Board initiated a registered public offering of an amount up to $35 million of Trust Preferred Capital Securities (more TruPS) in an underwritten public offering. This TruPS offering was withdrawn in June 2008 as market conditions for new bank capital continued to deteriorate, and it became clear that there was no investor appetite for more TruPS.

June 26, 2008 (AWBC Stock $ 2.00): U.S. Senator Schumer (D-NY) wrote a letter to bank regulators questioning the viability of IndyMac Bank, F.S.B., one of the nation's largest home lenders based in Pasadena, California. The letter became public and started a two-week, $1.3 billion run on IndyMac, culminating with national television coverage of long lines of depositors outside the IndyMac offices waiting to withdraw their deposits – the nation was witnessing a classic bank run for the first time since the 1930's.

July 11, 2008: IndyMac was closed on Friday and all of the non-brokered insured deposit accounts were transferred to a new bridge bank owned by the FDIC. No buyer was located for IndyMac and uninsured deposits were not covered in the transfer.

The Wall Street crisis had now come to Main Street and many banks, including AmericanWest, experienced significant deposit withdrawals.

July 24, 2008 (AWBC Stock $2.45): The Company reported a net loss of $6 million for the second quarter and a net loss of $38 million for the first six months of 2008.

Total non-performing assets had increased to $73 million or 3.44% of total assets at June 30, 2008, as compared to 2.30% at March 31, 2008 and 1.90% of total assets at December 31, 2007. Foreclosed assets at June 30, 2008 totaled $3 million and consisted of ten properties, as compared to $2 million and six properties at March 31, 2008. Time would show that this was just the beginning of the Bank's asset quality problems.

Total tangible shareholders' equity at the Company was $128 million and the tangible equity ratio was 6.4% at June 30. The Company and the Bank were now only "adequately capitalized" by regulatory standards and expected to be subject to a Supervisory Directive to raise additional capital.

The Company announced in its July earnings release that it had engaged Sandler O'Neill to serve as its financial advisor with respect to raising additional capital and evaluating other strategic alternatives, and that the previously announced public offering of up to $35 million of capital securities had been suspended due to adverse capital markets conditions for TruPS.

In addition, the Company announced that the Board of Directors had directed management to complete a comprehensive review of AmericanWest's operations to identify additional efficiencies and opportunities. The preliminary results of this review had determined that annualized pre-tax expense savings of $3 million could be realized through the consolidation of the Bank's commercial and retail banking delivery channels. The Company was also evaluating alternatives for improving operating performance and capital ratios through the sale of certain loans and the sale or consolidation of certain financial centers.

Rusnak, as Chief Operating Officer, stated in the release:

*"When it became apparent that current capital market conditions were not favorable to the issuance of capital securities, we quickly redirected efforts toward options in the new equity capital arena. Our presence in high-growth markets and deeply rooted core deposit franchise has attracted the attention of investors who can see beyond the horizon of the current credit cycle and appreciate the future earnings potential. We intend to pursue the evaluation and decision process for this recapitalization in a thoughtful but expedient manner."*

Regulators had just finished a regular exam of AmericanWest and the Bank was anticipating a

Supervisory Directive from the Washington Department of Financial Institutions (WDFI).

July 29, 2008 (AWBC Stock $1.50) AmericanWest announced that Daugherty had resigned as President and Chief Executive Officer at the request of the Company's Board of Directors. Patrick J. Rusnak was appointed Interim President and Chief Executive Officer. In the announcement, the Company's Chairman of the Board stated, *"Given our current financial positioning and the need for a meaningful change in our strategic vision, our board decided that an executive management change was in the company's best interests."*

In late July the capital markets for all bank stocks were in near chaos. The total market capitalization of AmericanWest had declined to $25 million, a decline in shareholder value of almost $300 million in the past seven months. Any issuance of new shares to raise additional equity capital, if it was even possible, would be highly dilutive.

# # #

Before continuing, I think it's important to note that from July 2008 on Rusnak's focus was always forward, not backward. I never heard Rusnak in public or private criticize anyone for the decisions and actions that eventually led to the Bank's increasingly dire circumstances.

Rusnak was always focused on what needed to be done to resolve problems, not looking for someone to blame. I believe his professional attitude helped create the positive forward-looking attitude exhibited by his entire management team.

# Chapter Five

# Interim Chief Executive

One of the first challenges encountered by any bank board facing a regulatory enforcement order is the requirement that all changes in executive management require regulatory approval. As a result, boards find it difficult to recruit new executives, and even an internal "promotion" requires regulatory approval.

At the same time, bank regulators expect prompt corrective action to be undertaken to by both the board and management of a troubled institution to address the issues identified in a regulatory order. AmericanWest was issued a "Supervisory Directive" from the WDFI on August 11, 2008, that required the Bank to provide periodic liquidity and credit reports, update the WDFI on the status of liquidity and capital planning, notify the WDFI about significant changes in management and financial condition, and retain a permanent Chief Executive Officer.

The Company's Board of Directors had confidence in Rusnak as a Chief Operating Officer and Chief Financial Officer, but he was relatively young and was unproven as a Chief Executive Officer. For these and other reasons, the Board believed that it was appropriate to conduct an executive search for a new CEO, and initiated the process in August of 2008.

As time progressed and the directors observed Rusnak's decisions, actions and leadership, it became increasingly clear to them that Rusnak was an appropriate choice to become the permanent CEO. However, it was not certain the Bank's regulators would approve Rusnak as the permanent CEO, and it's always unclear how much authority an interim CEO can exercise until regulatory approval is obtained.

Note: It was not until early October that the WDFI and FDIC would indicate that they did not object (their term for approval) to Rusnak's permanent appointment as CEO.

However, time was of the essence and Rusnak does not waste time.

*"Charles, this is Pat, I would like you to fly to Spokane."*

I accepted Rusnak's invitation and Chartwell Capital was retained as a financial advisor in early August to assist AmericanWest with liquidity and capital planning. In early 2007 Chartwell had been retained by another bank located in the Midwest to conduct our first Management Study as required by a regulatory order for that bank. This earlier project and other assignments combined with my selection as Chairman of the American Association of Bank Directors had provided unique insight into the approach of bank regulators and the management of operating issues faced by banks operating under regulatory orders.

Upon my arrival in Spokane, Rusnak met me at the airport in his pickup truck and drove to the Bank's Support Center to be introduced to the key people on his financial management team.

The Support Center became the center for management activity. It was months before I realized that Rusnak also had access to the prior CEO's large corner office in the Bank's downtown headquarters. To my knowledge he never moved into that corner office – he was too busy.

Rusnak was completely focused on the job at hand and started working from his small office along the south wall in the finance section of the Support Center. The Controller and Treasurer occupied the two larger corner offices on the floor just a few feet away. Based on the size of his office, any casual visitor would have mistaken Rusnak for a staff accountant – not the CEO.

Photo: Williams
Rusnak in his Support Center office

The financial staff at the Support Center became my working family in Spokane. They were at the center of action and knew the significance of the regulatory issues, so it was obviously a very stressful situation for all of them. I was constantly amazed at the positive attitudes exhibited by everyone in the group. To me, it was obvious this positive attitude was due to Rusnak's positive work ethic and leadership, as well as the leadership of his key financial executives.

Shelly Krasselt, Senior Vice President & Controller, managed all aspects of financial reporting and the accounting functions. Krasselt and her staff are the unsung heroes of the past three years. She and her team worked tirelessly to produce endless financial reports for management, regulators and potential investors. The work of Krasselt and her team was always accurate and professionally done, and I quickly learned you could completely rely on their work product.

Photo: Williams
Shelly Krasselt, Controller

Krasselt appears rather young for her position, and at one time I was asked by a potential investor to describe her professional capability – I answered, "Shelly requires no adult supervision. She knows her job and her work is excellent."

Linda Williams, Senior Vice President & Treasurer, managed liquidity and all aspects of planning, including asset/liability management. Williams quickly became the "go to" person for the vast majority of financial projects.

Williams was very skilled at interpreting vague ideas and producing financial models that provided Rusnak and me with the ability to test alternatives and assumptions, and to analyze potential results. She guided the asset/liability management process that provided the forecasts Rusnak could depend on for making critical decisions.

Every potential investor wanted to understand the Bank's potential for future profitability. All of the forecasting work fell on Williams and her team. They endured both stupid questions from MBAs who didn't have a clue about banking as well as probing interrogations from sophisticated investors.

Photo: Combs
Linda Williams, Treasurer

The focus of this book is to highlight the work done to recapitalize the Bank; however, both Krasselt and Williams devoted countless hours to answering questions for potential investors, attending meetings and preparing reports for bank regulators. The paperwork associated with a bank regulatory order is beyond comprehension.

## Liquidity Management

Liquidity was the first order of business, but it needs to be made very clear that all of the other actions described in this chapter occurred simultaneously. It was the start of a very challenging time.

The fallout from IndyMac had contributed to $50 million of deposit withdrawals at AmericanWest, and balance sheet liquidity had declined from $100 million to about $50 million for a time – too close for comfort. Rusnak and his team had already taken steps to apply to the Federal Reserve Bank (FED) "discount window" and to expand their borrowing capacity at the Federal Home Loan Bank (FHLB).

The most immediate challenge to be faced by the Bank was related to $250 million of maturing brokered Certificates of Deposit (CDs). The Federal Deposit Insurance Corporation Improvement Act (FDICIA) passed by Congress in 1991 following the last banking crisis had established new capital standards and steps ("prompt corrective action") that were to be taken by regulators and bank management when capital ratios fell below the established benchmarks.

At the time this legislation was enacted in 1991 the "adequate" capital category was intended to provide regulatory flexibility and not be a trigger for punitive measures. One such feature was the ability for a bank to request and receive a waiver that would permit the bank to issue new brokered CDs to replace maturing broker CDs. AmericanWest made such a request but based on my previous experience, approval was not anticipated.

The unpublished FDIC policy of not approving brokered CD waivers for "adequately capitalized" banks, in my view, reflects a serious lack of understanding at the FDIC concerning the reality of available funding for community banks. Adequately capitalized community banks are forced to replace maturing brokered CDs by increasing their share of deposits in their local markets. Paying more for local deposits than your competitors pay is the only way for a community bank to shift share of market. The net result is an increase in the cost of money for all community banks in that bank's home market – a terrible economic outcome for every bank in the market.

I had previously shared this view with senior officials at the FDIC, to no avail. No additional exposure is created to the FDIC's Deposit Insurance Fund (FDIC Fund) when maturing insured brokered CDs are replaced with new insured brokered CDs rather than insured local deposits; however, unnecessary liquidity failures do create losses for the Deposit Insurance Fund. I now find it interesting that some regulatory officials have acknowledged that many of the early failures were caused by lack of liquidity – not asset quality and lack of capital.

Furthermore, regulatory interest rate caps are imposed on troubled banks that are being forced to replace brokered deposits by obtaining deposits in their home markets. It was clear to any banker on the front lines that many community banks were facing their own liquidity crisis, and regulatory policy was not helping – FDIC policy was a contributor to both higher local funding costs and the liquidity problem.

It was in this economic and regulatory environment that the Bank faced the challenge of replacing $250 million of brokered deposits. If the funding currently provided by the outstanding brokered deposits was ignored, then the Bank had negative net liquidity in excess of $150 million!

The maturity schedule of the brokered deposits provided only a few months to implement a plan to both reduce assets and increase core deposits. Rusnak brought immediate focus to the management of liquidity and it became the most important daily measure. A daily liquidly report was circulated to all key managers – everyone knew what was needed and expected.

ALCO and the Treasury staff served as the navigation center for financial forecasting and future management strategy. Accurate financial forecasts provided by key mangers are essential for executive management to anticipate and avoid financial storms - just as the Captain of a ship at sea requires an accurate weather forecast to avoid storms. I observed a management team that understood forecasting was about accuracy, not unattainable goals. The ALCO team clearly helped navigate the Bank through the financial hurricane of 2008-09.

Members of the Bank's Asset/Liability Committee (ALCO) focused their attention on balance sheet forecasting and liquidity. Williams shared back test results with all ALCO members and forecasting consistently improved.

## AmericanWest Liquidity

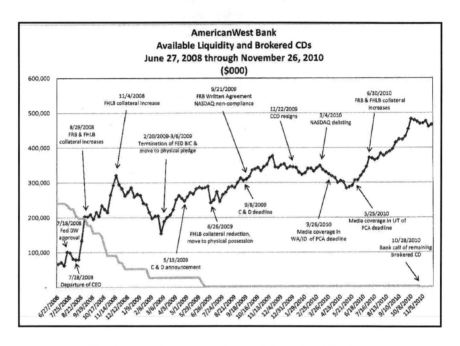

Chart reproduced courtesy of AmericanWest

The chart above illustrates the success of the liquidity story - one of the most significant management achievements at AmericanWest. The dark line represents total liquidity and the light grey line represents outstanding brokered CDs. Most important, the focus for the newly restructured branch management network was deposit retention and growth, not loan growth. AmericanWest was fortunate to have a strong branch network and great branch personnel in multiple markets located in Washington, Idaho and Utah. The execution of the deposit marketing plans by Nicole Sherman (Chief Banking Officer for Utah), Bob Harris (Chief Banking Officer for Washington & Idaho) and the Bank's branch personnel throughout the system was amazing.

Rusnak had frequent conference calls with all employees to explain any news (good and bad), regulatory issues, management's objectives, and to answer questions. There was a clear positive reaction to Rusnak's open style of leadership.

As a result of this powerful team effort, when the agreement to recapitalize the Bank was announced in October 2010, total net liquidity was over $450 million - management had achieved a $600+ million liquidity improvement in just over two years time!

Three other areas also required immediate and simultaneous attention.

### Special Assets Management

As interim CEO, Rusnak now had full responsibility for credit and asset quality. Steps were taken to strengthen risk management with the addition of a new Credit & Risk Committee at the Board level and the addition of staff to the Special Assets Division (SAD).

SAD had the very difficult job of resolving the Bank's problem loans and selling the Bank's foreclosed properties. Rusnak located the SAD group (no pun intended) adjacent to the financial staff at the Support Center. He didn't manage from a corporate tower - every critical function was close at hand at the Support Center.

The financial staff worked with SAD to develop a problem loan migration analysis that would provide management with a comprehensive analysis of monthly migration trends. This analysis would serve as the forecasting tool to better anticipate future credit trends.

Rusnak set the "Tone at the Top" for recognition of loan losses. Problems were addressed quickly - not ignored. "It Is What It Is" was the credit philosophy that established credibility with both regulators and investors.

### Organizational Assessment

Rusnak and the management team had previously completed a strategic reassessment of the Bank's business plan and methods of doing business, and had identified alternatives for improving the Bank's performance. The recommendations from this recent organizational analysis would now be expanded upon and put into action. The organization was streamlined to both improve customer service and achieve annual cost savings of $6 million (double the predicted savings mentioned in July press release).

### Capital Plan

The regulatory orders required the Bank to submit a Capital Restoration Plan (CRP) with updates as time passed. It's difficult to prepare a realistic plan that requires new capital when the capital markets are essentially closed for business. Hope is not considered a valid plan by bank regulators.

Our approach was to consider every alternative that could improve the Bank's capital ratios. The plan submitted would leave no stone unturned.

The capital plan contained alternatives for the issuance of all forms of securities that qualified as regulatory capital, asset reduction strategies, branch divestitures and bank-level capital alternatives.

The bank-level alternatives initially considered the creation of a subsidiary of the Bank to own the

Bank's non-performing assets. The objective was not to remove the assets from the Bank's financial statements but rather a technique to add capital in the form of preferred stock at the loan subsidiary level. This new subsidiary and the additional capital would then be consolidated with the Bank's financial statements and thereby increase the Bank's consolidated capital position. This rather complex arrangement had previously been approved by bank regulators and utilized by two of Chartwell's other clients in the Midwest.

As will be described in subsequent chapters, the concept of a bank-level recapitalization was initiated eighteen months later in a completely different form.

## Loan Sales

Bank regulators actually focus on a bank's capital ratios rather than the dollar amount of capital. Therefore capital ratios can be improved by either the addition of new capital or a reduction in assets. With the capital markets essentially closed, it was logical to consider a reduction in assets as an alternative strategy.

Unfortunately, an asset reduction strategy doesn't make economic sense – the only assets than can be sold are high quality performing assets – this includes a bank's most profitable loans. Successful implementation of loan sales as a capital strategy creates a less profitable bank. This is another example of the unintended consequences created by regulatory action.

In any event, other banks were not interested in buying loans from AmericanWest. Loan growth was not on the agenda for other banks - they were concerned about credit risk, their next regulatory exam and maintaining their own regulatory capital ratios. The reduction in the AmericanWest loan portfolio was largely the result of maturing loans.

## Branch Divesture Strategy

Several departments in the Bank – Finance, Facilities, Operations, Marketing and Human Resources - undertook an extensive branch-by-branch analysis to identify clusters of branches for the possible sale of performing loans and deposits. Marketing materials were developed for several clusters of branches ranging between $150 million and $350 million in size. Such a transaction would enhance the Bank's capital ratios and permit the Bank to focus on its remaining markets.

On a proforma basis, each reduction of $100 million of assets and deposits achieved through branch sales at a 5% deposit premium would have improved the Bank's capital position by approximately $15 million, which would have increased the Bank's total risk-based capital ratio by approximately 80 basis points.

During 2008 and 2009, Chartwell Capital had worked successfully with several of its Midwest banking clients to execute capital strategies that included multiple branch sale transactions. We were initially optimistic that AmericanWest could execute a similar strategy, and Glowasky was negotiating a potential transaction with an out-of-state acquiror that assured us that regulatory approval would not be a problem. That assurance came before that bank received the results of its most recent regulatory examination. Bank regulators would not approve the proposed transaction, and the FDIC ultimately seized the other bank.

These projects and more were all underway as Rusnak and his management team entered September 2008 – had we known then of the financial hurricane that was coming in September we may not have been quite so positive in our outlook.

# # #

The focus of this book is management's actions in response to regulatory requirements and market conditions. However, it's important to acknowledge the commitment and support provided by every member of the Board of Directors throughout the process of enhancing liquidity, resolving problem credits and raising needed capital. The Bank's Directors were faced with some very tough decisions and they acted courageously.

## Chapter Six

## Financial Meltdown

It's probably best none of us had time to watch television. This is the first financial crisis covered hour-by-hour on national television. In my opinion, the all-day business coverage on CNBC and other news channels had a significant negative impact on public confidence – and liquidity runs are created by a lack of confidence. The business and other news channels all appeared to be competing with one another to deliver the latest market rumor and self fulfilling bad news.

The events of September 2008 have been covered in great detail by numerous articles and books, so this section will not cover unnecessary ground. The point is to illustrate the market conditions that were unfolding as Rusnak and his management team were restructuring the Bank.

September 7, 2008: The Federal Housing Finance Agency (FHFA) placed Fannie Mae and Freddie Mac, two government-sponsored enterprises (GSEs) that play a critical role in the U.S. home mortgage market, into conservatorship. As conservator, the FHFA had full power to control the assets and operations of the firms.

Dividends for common and preferred shareholders were suspended, but the U.S. Treasury put in place a set of financing agreements to ensure that the GSEs continued to meet their obligations to holders of the bonds they issued or guaranteed. The U.S. taxpayer now stood behind about $5 trillion of GSE debt.

Government officials reported this step was taken because a default by either of the two institutions, which had been battered by the downturn in housing and credit markets, would have caused severe disruptions in global financial markets, made home mortgages more difficult and expensive to obtain, and produced negative repercussions throughout the nation's economy.

Fortunately, AmericanWest had a relatively small investment portfolio and unlike many community banks owned no GSE preferred stock. The decision to suspend dividends on the GSE preferred shares sent shockwaves through the capital markets – these shares had been considered "bank eligible" investments until the day the government decided to stop payment. Numerous community banks took a serious hit to their capital positions with no regulatory help in sight.

September 15, 2008: On Monday morning, one week later, Lehman Brothers filed for bankruptcy following a massive exodus of liquidity, loss of clients, a dramatic decline in stock value and the devaluation of its assets by the rating agencies the prior week. Lehman was the largest bankruptcy in U.S. history. The market was well aware that Lehman was in trouble and was expecting some type of resolution, but not bankruptcy. The global impact was beyond comprehension. Allowing Lehman to descend to bankruptcy may have been the worst decision made during the entire financial crisis.

September 25, 2008: Lehman Brothers was followed ten days later by the seizure of Washington Mutual (WAMU) on a Thursday after the bank experienced the withdrawal of over $16 billion in deposits during what was described as a 10-day bank run reflecting a significant loss of depositor confidence following the GSE and Lehman announcements.

Washington Mutual was the sixth largest bank in the nation with over $300 billion of deposits, and was the largest bank failure in American financial history. Fortunately, unlike IndyMac, the FDIC had a buyer this time, and JP Morgan reopened the bank the next day as JP Morgan Chase offices.

September 29, 2008: On Monday morning the FDIC announced that following weekend negotiations, Citibank was acquiring Wachovia in an "open bank" transaction with financial support provided by the FDIC. Market reaction was confused, and the confusion was further compounded when the FDIC permitted Wells Fargo to propose another approach to the transaction within days. Ultimately, after a public legal battle, Wells Fargo acquired Wachovia. The FDIC's actions and the uncertain outcome of the transaction further unsettled the financial markets.

Wachovia, the fourth largest bank, had suffered a significant stock decline and reported withdrawals of $5.0 billion of deposits following the failure of Washington Mutual. Wachovia's credit problems were related to its acquisition of Golden West, the second largest savings & loan in the nation, in May 2006. Golden West had specialized in option ARM loans marketed under the name "Pick-A-Pay," a product now considered toxic by the credit markets.

In just one short month, the nation had witnessed the government takeover of two government sponsored mortgage institutions (including the taxpayer guarantee of $5 trillion in GSE debt), the largest bankruptcy in the nation's history with Lehman Brothers, the largest bank failure in the nation's history at WAMU, and the near failure of Wachovia, the nation's fourth largest bank.

These external problems were producing terrible headlines at a time when AmericanWest was facing its own internal challenges, including building liquidity, undertaking major organizational changes, identifying more problem loans, making preparations to report another significant quarterly loss ($97 million), and attempting to raise new capital.

This was definitely not a good environment for AmericanWest to report more bad news!

## Chapter Seven

## Government Response

October 3, 2008: The Troubled Asset Relief Program (TARP) was signed into law. The program was originally intended to purchase or insure up to $700 billion of troubled assets from financial institutions. Much has been written about TARP (mostly negative) but the announcement of the program did offer some hope at a difficult time for AmericanWest.

October 8, 2008: The government of Iceland freezes the banking assets of Landsbanki, Icesave (Landsbanki's United Kingdom subsidiary with $7 billion of UK customer deposits) and the Iceland Central Bank. The global impact of the financial meltdown was increasingly evident.

October 14, 2008: After a false start, the TARP program was converted into a Capital Purchase Program (CPP) that was introduced with the announcement that the nine largest banks were participating in the program. The original concept of purchasing troubled assets sounded good, but proved far too complicated to implement.

Based on the formula provided in the CPP, AmericanWest was eligible for up to $57 million in CPP investment, and the Bank submitted an application to participate in the CPP program. The addition of CPP capital, even without private investment or branch or asset sales, would not only assure that the Bank would be well-capitalized, but would also enable it to more actively continue to extend credit, while at the same time continue to resolve its credit quality issues.

As a precaution, the Board and management elected to continue their capital-raising program after the announcement of the CPP even though the Bank would have been "well-capitalized" at that time with the addition of $57 million of CPP alone.

The approval process for community banks to participate in the CPP program was clouded in bureaucratic doublespeak. The key issue was whether a community bank needed to be viable before or after a CPP investment. In the case of AmericanWest, regulatory guidance indicated that an application would be approvable only if the CPP investment was matched by an equal amount of private capital investment.

Photo: Glowasky
Al Glowasky

With that understanding in hand, Glowasky and his team worked the phones to identify potential investment partners for the CPP program. Glowasky already had discussions underway with several potential investors - an amazing accomplishment considering recent events and the ugly investment environment.

Over the next several months, Rusnak and Glowasky executed non-disclosure agreements with over 30 private equity firms or hedge funds, 5 accredited investors and 4 financial institutions in order for these organizations to conduct due diligence. As a result of these efforts, the Company received term sheets from private equity firms in both December 2008 and January 2009 outlining proposals to purchase securities that qualified as regulatory capital.

October 31, 2008 (AWBC Stock $1.25): The Company released its third quarter financial results and reported a net loss of $97 million, as compared to a net loss of $6 million for the second quarter of 2008. For the nine months ending September 30, 2008, the Company reported a net loss of $135 million as compared to net income of $12 million for the same period of the prior year. AWBC Stock was essentially unchanged following the announcements.

Included in the third quarter 2008 results was a non-cash goodwill impairment charge of $82 million; a similar charge of $27 million was recognized in the first quarter of 2008. These non-cash impairment charges had no impact on the Company's regulatory capital or liquidity position. However, media coverage focused on the $135 million loss.

The Company also announced it had deferred dividend payments on $40 million of TruPS, resulting in additional annual retention of $3 million of capital.

As of September 30, 2008, the Company and the Bank were "adequately capitalized" by regulatory standards. The capital shortfall to qualify as "well capitalized" for the Bank was approximately $14 million.

On a more positive note, the Board announced the Bank had completed a comprehensive review of its operations with the following statement:

*In connection with completion of this review, the Company has appointed key executive management personnel to ensure the prompt and successful* implementation of a more streamlined business model, improved capital ratios and a reduction in the level of non-performing assets. AmericanWest Bank also announces that it will participate in the FDIC's program to insure all non-interest bearing deposits without passing any related costs to customers.

### Executive Management Appointments

The Company's board of directors has received regulatory approval for the appointment of Patrick J. Rusnak as permanent President and Chief Executive Officer. Mr. Rusnak joined AmericanWest in September 2006 as Executive Vice President and Chief Operating Officer, and has served as interim President and Chief Executive Officer since July 2008. Mr. Rusnak has over 20 years of banking experience, including serving in executive management roles at Western Sierra Bancorp, Umpqua Holdings Corporation and Humboldt Bancorp.

"We believe Pat Rusnak is uniquely qualified to provide the leadership necessary to improve operating performance," remarked Craig D. Eerkes, Chairman of the Board. "He has the clarity of vision, ability to make tough decisions and resourceful approach to leadership necessary to resolve the challenges currently facing our company. These qualities, combined with Pat's firsthand knowledge of our bank's strengths and weaknesses, give us confidence that our bank's streamlined business model will be implemented quickly and successfully."

The Board of Directors has also appointed Nicole Sherman to the position of Executive Vice President and Chief Banking Officer for its Utah markets. Ms. Sherman joined AmericanWest in December 2005 as Director of Retail Banking. Prior to joining the Company, Ms. Sherman held a variety of management positions for Zions Bank in the Salt Lake City area. Her prior experience in the Utah market combined with her banking knowledge and expertise provides the leadership required in this important market.

"Nicole knows our company and she knows the Utah market," Rusnak commented. "Our Utah franchise is large and unique enough that it merits the full-time focus of a dedicated executive officer. We are confident that Nicole's experience and leadership abilities will help ensure that our new business plan is successfully implemented in that important part of our franchise."

### Organizational Changes

The executive management team presented and received approval for its revised business plan from the Board of Directors at a series of September meetings. The plan includes a revised organizational structure that strengthens risk management and streamlines the Company's overall management structure. The central focus of the Company's revised business model is the consolidation of its retail banking, commercial banking and private banking delivery channels into a single channel focused on community banking.

The implementation of this revised business model is being launched today, with the internal announcement of the above-referenced executive management changes, under which the Company's banking operations report to a single executive in each of its two principal markets.

"Current economic conditions required us to undertake a complete reevaluation of the previous delivery model with an eye to improving customer satisfaction and streamlining staffing levels to generate improved financial performance," said Rusnak. "We are returning to a tried-and-true approach to community banking, with empowered local managers who are focused on business banking. We are confident this model will provide customers with the same, if not greater, level of superior service they are accustomed to. We have worked hard to ensure a seamless transition."

*The Company expects this streamlined business model will result in annualized pre-tax non-interest expense savings of approximately $4.9 million upon completion of the implementation, which is expected by year-end 2008. A pre-tax charge to cover employee severance related expense of approximately $670 thousand is expected to be recognized, a majority of which will be during the fourth quarter of 2008.*

### Performance Improvement Initiatives

*During the third quarter of 2008, management completed a review of the Company's 64 financial centers and identified six that did not currently meet, and were not likely to meet in the future, targeted performance levels, or that were in such close proximity to other centers that the two could easily be combined and maintain service levels. As a result of this review, the Company has initiated the process to formally close the following financial centers: Edison, Latah, Oakesdale, Qualchan, St. Maries (in-store) and West Plains. All customer accounts currently domiciled in these financial centers will be automatically transferred to nearby AmericanWest financial centers.*

*"Like the decision to streamline our business model, the decision to consolidate financial centers was the subject of careful consideration and review," commented Rusnak.*

*The closure of financial centers is subject to statutory notice periods and, accordingly, management expects the consolidations will be completed during the first quarter of 2009. The Company expects these consolidations will result in initial annualized pre-tax expense savings of approximately $650 thousand, with an additional $350 thousand of annual savings realized upon the disposition of related facilities. During the fourth quarter of 2008, the Company anticipates recording approximately $80 thousand of pre-tax employee related severance costs associated with these* closures. In addition, the Company has consolidated office space in its headquarters building and entered into a sublease effective October 1, 2008 that will reduce annual premises expense by approximately $200 thousand.

The Company will be working closely with local community leaders to ensure that any adverse impacts of the closures are minimized and will evaluate the feasibility of providing financial incentives for the bank facilities to be utilized under economic redevelopment initiatives.

# # #

It had been a very busy first 90 days!

## Chapter Eight

## Big Hat – No Cattle

Over the coming months Glowasky and his associates would work the phones, arrange meetings, sign non-disclosure agreements, arrange due diligence and successfully negotiate several term sheets.

A wide variety of investors were involved in these discussions. They ranged from hedge funds that sent very inexperienced MBAs who didn't have a clue about analyzing a troubled bank to very experienced investors that had participated in bank recapitalizations in the early 1990's.

The most frustrating were the potential investors that had a blend of experience, as it was nearly impossible to determine if they really knew what they were doing in a very uncertain economic and investment environment.

I was raised in the Midwest and we had a saying about want-to-be cowboys – they always looked the part (Big Hat) but owned no cattle. Many of the potential investors talked a good story (Big Hat) but most lacked the financial capacity (No Cattle) to complete a transaction.

Glowasky worked hard and managed to circle over $30 million of capital from qualified investors. This was a frustrating amount – a significant level but not enough to close the existing regulatory shortfall or to match $57 million of CPP. Without a sufficient amount of new capital to match CPP, no investor was willing to make a commitment.

Regulatory and legal requirements relating to bank ownership also presented a significant investment hurdle. In simple terms, almost any investor can own up to 4.9% of a bank. The ownership requirements get increasingly complex if an investor increases its ownership to 10% and higher. Significant ownership interest required regulatory approval.

The most significant threshold is 25% - any investor owning more than 24.9% must become a registered bank holding company. There are numerous restrictions on the other activities that a registered financial holding company may conduct.

In addition, there is a significant financial commitment - a registered bank holding company must serve as a "source of strength" to any subsidiary bank. The risk of loss to an investor who owns stock in any other company is typically limited to the investor's investment, but an institutional investor that owns more than 25% of a bank is subject to additional loss. For example, if an institutional investor were to own 25% of a bank that was failing, bank regulators could demand that additional capital be invested in the bank by that investor.

Therefore, most institutional investors want to avoid registration as a bank holding company, and therefore choose to limit their ownership interest in any one transaction. The net result was the need for Glowasky to obtain commitments from as many as 21 separate investors so that each would own less than 5% and not be subject to excessive regulatory conditions.

On the other hand, a number of investment funds were being organized to become registered bank holding companies and would have the authority to acquire control of individual banks. Not only was this a complex and time consuming process, but the FDIC required even higher capital commitments and higher capital ratios from these new funds. These higher capital requirements would lower potential investment returns. Such regulatory roadblocks did nothing to encourage new investment in banks like AmericanWest.

2008 ended on an ugly note - the Company reported a net loss of $192 million, primarily as the result of $97 million provision for loan losses and $109 million in goodwill impairment. Non-performing assets were over $100 million and exceeded tangible capital. Tangible bank capital ended 2008 at $ 97 million. The Bank was now considered "under-capitalized" by the FDIC.

The best news was the almost $400 million improvement in total liquidity! The management team at AmericanWest had succeeded in building a solid foundation of liquidity during the nation's worst financial meltdown since the 1930's Depression.

**AmericanWest Bank: 2008**

| $ million | 1Q08 | 2Q08 | 3Q08 | 4Q08 |
|---|---|---|---|---|
| Assets | $2,106 | $2,107 | $1,988 | $1,872 |
| Loans | $1,747 | $1,748 | $1,694 | $1,589 |
| Capital (a) | $ 173 | $ 167 | $ 153 | $ 97 |
| NPA | $ 48 | $ 73 | $ 89 | $ 108 |
| Liquidity (b) | - | $ - 175 | $ 38 | $ 220 |
| Capital % (c) | 8.71 % | 8.38 % | 7.82 % | 5.28 % |

(a) Bank Tangible Capital
(b) Total Liquidity Net of Broker CDs
(c) Tangible Assets divided by Tangible Capital

In addition, the Company had received a non-binding indication from the FDIC that its application to issue $57 million of preferred stock under the CPP would be forwarded to the Treasury with a recommendation for approval, subject to the Company receiving an equivalent amount of private equity. The liquidity cushion would provide Rusnak and Glowasky with time to negotiate the required capital investment.

December 31, 2008 (AWBC Stock $.75): An additional $46 million of capital was needed by the Bank to meet the requirements to be considered well-capitalized. The regulatory order being proposed by the WDFI and FDIC would require $80 million of additional capital to achieve a 10% Tier 1 leverage capital ratio.

The Company's 10K for 2008 (published March 31, 2009) disclosed pages of discouraging risk factors to investors including:

**The Company may not be able to continue to operate as a going concern.**

The Company has determined that significant additional sources of liquidity and capital will likely be required to continue operations in the future.

**The Company is required to raise additional capital, but that capital may not be available.**

The Company and the Bank are required by federal regulatory authorities to maintain adequate levels of capital to support operations. If the Company cannot raise additional capital the Bank may be subjected to additional adverse regulatory action.

**The Company's liquidity could be impaired by an inability to access the capital markets or an unforeseen outflow of cash.**

Liquidity is essential to the Company's business and it relies on external sources to finance a significant portion of operations. Due to circumstances that the Company may be unable to control, such as a general capital markets disruption or negative news about banks generally, liquidity could be impaired by an inability to access the capital markets, an unforeseen outflow of cash due to depositor withdrawals or a disruption in lending programs of the FRB or FHLB.

***The Company may be subject to additional regulatory enforcement action that could place significant restrictions on the Company's operations.***

*Under applicable laws, the FDIC and the WDFI have the ability to impose substantial sanctions, restrictions and requirements on the Bank if they determine, upon examination or otherwise, violations of laws with which the Company must comply, or weaknesses or failures with respect to general standards of safety and soundness.*

*Failure to adhere to the requirements, if imposed,* ***could result in more severe restrictions including seizure of the Bank.***

# # #

Ever hopeful and personally dedicated to the assignment, Glowasky and his team continued their efforts to locate new investors as the Bank entered 2009.

# Chapter Nine

# *Groundhog Day*

The year 2009 opened with record monthly snowfall in Spokane – over 10 feet! My frequent visits were marked by a 7 A.M. pickup at the hotel by Rusnak in his pickup truck. Our days were spent at the Support Center working on multiple projects, but mostly focused on capital strategy and exploring every alternative available to obtain new capital. The days seldom ended before 9 P.M. These were typical days for Rusnak – the reason this book is dedicated to his family.

Photo: Williams
The CEO and his pickup truck in the snow

The September reorganization had streamlined the Company's operations and Rusnak had been approved as CEO. However, he still wore multiple "hats" as he continued to serve as the Company's CFO. Shelly Krasselt, Controller, and Linda Williams, Treasurer, were quickly stepping up to expanded responsibilities and all required work was being accomplished. I directed some of my efforts to serving as a "CFO consultant" and worked with Krasselt and Williams on a few strategic issues. However, Rusnak had a solid financial team and little guidance was actually required.

Therefore, once at the Support Center, I focused my efforts on special projects with the assistance of the Finance and Accounting staff. Rusnak and I did not attend many meetings together – we didn't need to duplicate efforts. Most evenings we would debrief at a small, quiet restaurant near the hotel and plan our schedule for the following day. We didn't exhibit much imagination in our work routine together – Rusnak just focused on getting results.

Photo: Williams
Support Center was Action Central

I did find time for an occasional after dinner walk. Downtown Spokane is surprisingly busy with several renovated hotels, a number of nice restaurants, a modern shopping complex and students from nearby Gonzaga University. I especially enjoyed walking through the park along the Spokane River.

When I was not in Spokane, my day would frequently start with an early morning call from Rusnak – remember the time zones, I live on the east coast.

Glowasky and his team continued to diligently work with potential investors and succeeded in getting close to but never across the goal line – the investment environment just "sucked."

In many respects 2009 reminded me of the movie "Groundhog Day" where the main character wakes up each morning to the same day – he is stuck in a time warp.

The good news was again the Bank's liquidity. The success of the Bank's branch employees in working with their customers to maintain and build the core deposit base was the foundation for the Bank's constantly improving liquidity position. Strong liquidity continued to provide Rusnak and his management team with time to raise capital.

The bad news was the continued decline of the real estate market in Utah and its impact on the Bank's asset quality and capital position. During the year, NPAs increased to $159 million and tangible capital declined to $53 million. The Special Assets team was working hard at resolving problems and selling foreclosed properties but the inflow of newly identified problems was greater than the market for foreclosed property. Both NPAs and capital were headed in the wrong direction.

Rusnak was focused on providing the Board, his management team and potential investors with access to current information. The Bank had enhanced Board communication with a Board portal and established an online portal for more efficient investor due diligence.

The Bank also worked with an outside firm to develop a specialized system for the management of its special assets (SATrac) that provided current problem loan information to management, auditors, examiners and potential investors.

The "Groundhog Day" effect also applied to the efforts to identify and negotiate with potential investors.

The Bank was well prepared for investor due diligence. The secure online data room was well organized and contained all relevant information for investor due diligence.

During the previous eight months, management had executed non-disclosure agreements with over 40 potential investors in order for them to conduct due diligence.

The most recent independent third-party loan review engaged by the Bank had validated the Bank's internal loan grading and classifications. An independent loan review conducted by a national accounting firm on behalf of a potential investor had also confirmed these results. The numbers were bad, but they were accurate at a time when the market questioned everything and everybody.

Rusnak and his Credit Administration team were building important credibility with both the Bank's regulators and potential investors. The asset quality reports made it clear that the Bank's expansion into the Utah market, initiated by the previous CEO in 2006 prior to Rusnak's arrival, was the principal reason for the Bank's increase in non-performing assets.

Approximately $250 million of Utah real estate construction and development loans had been originated or acquired. While approximately 32% of the Bank's total loan portfolio was related to operations in the Utah market as of December 31, 2008, the Utah portfolio represented 60% of total non-performing assets as of that date. Many of these non-performing loans had been originated in the Bank's loan production office prior to the acquisition of Far West Bank.

AmericanWest had adopted a policy of recognizing charge-offs (rather than establishing specific reserves) when loan impairment was identified. This is a more conservative policy that recognizes loan losses earlier than banks that establish specific impairment reserves.

The Bank neither originated nor held sub-prime mortgage loans or related securities, and the Bank had no exposure to GSE preferred securities nor had the Bank invested in TruPS.

The Bank had not seen significant deterioration in its portfolio of home equity loans, and took proactive steps to assure continued asset quality in that portfolio. Among other things, the Bank initiated a review of home equity loans and reduced credit limits where appropriate and in accordance with regulatory requirements. Home equity loans comprise only 7.5% of the Bank's total loans.

The Bank also had limited exposure to possible deterioration in credit card loans, having sold its $3 million credit card portfolio in 2008. The purchaser of the portfolio continued to market credit cards to the Bank's customers in all the Bank's market areas, providing a source of referral income to the Bank with no credit risk.

Investors that conducted due diligence during 2009 were complimentary of the information provided and the efforts management had undertaken to manage asset quality – but investor sentiment remained awful.

February 2, 2009: The FDIC issued a Prompt Corrective Action Notification (PCA) to the Bank. The PCA advised the Bank that it was "significantly undercapitalized" and was required to submit a Capital Restoration Plan (CRP) and that it was subject to restrictions relating to its senior management team, management compensation, dividends, loan loss reserves, reductions in troubled assets, liquidity and asset growth.

February 26, 2009: The Obama Administration presented a dark economic scenario and announced plans for "Stress Tests" to be undertaken by the nation's largest banks. The Administration indicated that results of the stress tests could become the starting point for a significant new infusion of government capital into the banking system, if required, to withstand such a bleak economic scenario.

Markets had a negative reaction to the "Stress Test" announcement and the equity markets hit their low point in March 2009. AWBC traded as low as $.30 per share indicating a market value for the entire company of less than $6 million. Shares must trade above $1.00 to remain listed on NASDAQ and the Company faced being delisted.

April 22, 2009: Rusnak presented a status report on the Bank's financial condition to representatives of the Federal Reserve Bank in San Francisco, including an update on raising private capital to match CPP funding.

Following this meeting, AmericanWest received notice from the FDIC that the CPP program was being "wound down" and if the Company could not obtain commitments prior to the deadline for processing applications, that its application for the CPP should be withdrawn. The CPP alternative had reached a dead end.

April 28, 2009: AmericanWest notified the FDIC and Federal Reserve in writing of its decision to withdraw its CPP application. The opportunity for the Bank to match funds was now history and the full amount of new capital required would need to be obtained from private investors.

May 11, 2009: On May 8, the Bank agreed to a Stipulation and Consent with the FDIC and WDFI, and three days later the FDIC and WDFI issued an Order to Cease and Desist (Order) requiring, among other things, that the Bank develop and adopt, within 60 days, or by July 10, 2009, a plan to meet and maintain the minimum risk-based capital requirements by September 9, 2009.

Based on those documents, the Company announced on May 15 that the Bank had entered into a joint agreement with the FDIC and WDFI for an action plan designed to strengthen and improve the Bank's financial condition and operations.

Regulatory enforcement actions have a special language. Such terms as Supervisory Directive, Capital Restoration Plan, Consent Order and Prompt Corrective Action all have very specific definitions. As described earlier, a "No Objection" letter represents regulatory approval of a new executive officer.

Regulatory enforcement actions frequently require a bank's board to retain an independent third party to conduct a "Management Study". Such studies are to provide the bank's board and bank regulators with an independent assessment and recommendations for such areas as:

- The bank's board & management oversight structure
- The experience and qualifications of management
- Provide a plan to recruit new officers as needed

Such management studies are required when bank regulators question the adequacy of the bank's board oversight or the competence of the bank's management. Chartwell has conducted a series of such studies over the past four years. The fact that bank regulators did not require such a study at AmericanWest indicated to me, that even in such dire circumstances, that bank regulators supported the actions Rusnak and the Board were undertaking.

May 28, 2009: Following the withdrawal of the CPP application, the Board of Directors conducted a strategic review of capital market activity and AmericanWest's strategic alternatives with management and AmericanWest's financial advisors, Sandler O'Neill and Chartwell Capital.

In addition to issuing new capital at the holding company level, the Board of Directors reviewed alternative financial structures including: (1) divestiture of selected non-core branch locations with related deposits and loans, (2) new investment directly at the Bank level and (3) the formation of a liquidating subsidiary to hold the Bank's non-performing assets and serve as a conduit for additional Bank regulatory capital.

In addition, the Board reviewed a number of government-initiated programs, including increased limits for FDIC deposit insurance, which had been announced by bank regulators to enhance bank asset and deposit liquidity. These enhanced deposit insurance limits proved very beneficial to AmericanWest.

AmericanWest had also explored participation in other government programs; however, participation in most programs required regulatory approval and was restricted to "well capitalized" banks. For example, the FDIC had previously indicated that the Company should withdraw its application to participate in the Debt Guarantee Program. It was another frustrating development. Frequent public announcements of selected government programs to assist all banks were frequently dead ends for community banks.

The Board of Directors continued to indicate its support for management's efforts to explore all potential alternatives to acquire the additional capital required by the Order. The Board's willingness to consider every alternative was an important contributor to the final structure adopted by AmericanWest.

The consequences of a recapitalization would be significant - based on the Company's current share price, new investment in excess of $100 million (the magnitude now required by the Order) would require the issuance of new shares representing over 90% ownership of the recapitalized Company. Any successful recapitalization would essentially represent the sale of the Company to new owners.

June 30, 2009: Tangible shareholders' equity for the Company was down to $35 million and the tangible equity ratio was 1.98%. The Company's consolidated regulatory capital ratios as of June 30, 2009 were in the "under capitalized" classification.

The Bank continued to pursue a possible branch sale in the summer of 2009. However, the FDIC informed the Bank that branch sales would not receive approval unless the sale was part of an overall transaction including the addition of new capital that would return the Bank to satisfactory regulatory capital levels. We had encountered another regulatory dead end.

This dead end was especially frustrating to me, as Chartwell had recently completed several branch transactions for banking clients in the Midwest that did not require the addition of new capital. In fact, Chartwell had been ranked #5 nationwide in 2008 and would be ranked #4 nationwide in 2009 for the number of bank branch transactions completed by all investment banking firms. Sandler O'Neill was ranked #1 for the number of branch transactions in both years.

During late summer, an institutional investor expressed interest in pursuing a bank-level investment by organizing and investing in a non-performing loan subsidiary of the Bank. Extensive negotiations were undertaken but two significant hurdles developed. First, it became clear the fund's investors were going to request unsupportable dividend payments. Second, feedback from the FDIC concerning similar transactions indicated they were no longer approving such structures. To add to the confusion, the structures were not being denied but were simply not being acted upon – just gathering dust until they were withdrawn. We had encountered another regulatory dead end.

That was the agonizing capital story of 2009 – one dead end after another – Groundhog Day.

There are always a multitude of personal stories in any organization with over 500 employees. The stress created by the Bank's capital position was seldom evident in day-to-day activity. Positive leadership certainly helps create a positive working atmosphere.

Shelly Krasselt took a short leave to have a baby and the entire financial staff shared in the excitement of a happy, healthy child. Anthony Gould, a financial consultant helping with accounting matters, was drafted to fill in while Krasselt was on leave. It should be noted that Gould was a frequent visitor to Spokane and played a key supporting role throughout 2009-10.

Everyone was deeply concerned when Wade Griffith, the Chief Information Officer, was diagnosed with cancer and all were very grateful when he was able to return to work at the Bank nearly a year later, after completing successful treatment. It was very evident to me that the people at AmericanWest not only worked well together; they also sincerely cared about one another as individuals.

As AmericanWest ended 2009 it was becoming increasingly clear that the most important capital ratio was the tangible equity ratio at the Bank. Washington State provides little flexibility to the WDFI; if the Bank's tangible capital ratio fell below 2.0% it would be seized by the WDFI and sold by the FDIC.

The Bank's liquidity continued to improve and now exceeded $300 million. This level of liquidity would provide the Bank's regulators with confidence that AmericanWest would not become a liquidity failure. The strong liquidity position continued to give management a little additional time to locate new investors and obtain needed capital.

**AmericanWest Bank: 2009**

| $ million | 1Q09 | 2Q09 | 3Q09 | 4Q09 |
|---|---|---|---|---|
| Assets | $1,823 | $1,776 | $1,762 | $1,654 |
| Loans | $1,536 | $1,452 | $1,352 | $1,238 |
| Capital (a) | $ 84 | $ 77 | $ 69 | $ 53 |
| NPA | $ 145 | $ 157 | $ 156 | $ 159 |
| Liquidity (b) | $ 204 | $ 238 | $ 322 | $ 342 |
| Capital % (c) | 4.70 % | 4.41 % | 3.96 % | 3.20% |

(a) Bank Tangible Capital
(b) Total Liquidity Net of Broker CDs
(c) Tangible Assets divided by Tangible Capital

December 31, 2009: The Bank's asset quality had continued to deteriorate during the year. The level of total non-performing assets had increased to $159 million. Other real estate owned (OREO or foreclosed property) had increased from $16 million to over $53 million during the year. The increase in foreclosed property reflected the actions being taken by Special Assets to resolve problem loans.

The Company's total tangible shareholders' equity was down to $9 million and the tangible equity ratio at the holding company was down to 0.5%.

The Bank's tangible capital had declined to $53 million and the capital ratio was down to 3.2%. The Bank was classified as "significantly undercapitalized" for regulatory capital purposes.

It should be explained at this point why the Bank's tangible capital ratios were higher than the Company's ratios. The $40 million of proceeds from the holding company's TruPS issues had been invested in the equity capital of the subsidiary Bank, so the Bank had $40 million of equity where the Company had $40 million in debt. It's this relationship that plays an important role in our story during 2010.

The Bank's tangible capital ratios were steadily declining. If tangible equity at the Bank declined below 2.0% then the WDFI was obligated by law to seize the Bank.

# # #

Time was short as AmericanWest entered 2010.

# Chapter Ten

# Dead End Detour

Another year had passed and with no capital in sight from traditional bank investors. Rusnak and I began the year by debating other alternatives.

An executive at another troubled bank had suggested Rusnak visit with a boutique investment banking firm located in Los Angeles. The firm had proposed approaching non-traditional bank investors as a source of new capital. That approach was of interest to us as Glowasky and his team had clearly contacted every potential traditional bank investor. Maybe a new approach to other potential investors had merit.

Glowasky and his team had made an amazing effort but had not yet produced enough commitments to complete an offering. Rusnak and I were concerned, however, that a change in investment bankers might confuse the market and not help locate new capital. We did not want a new person contacting potential investors who had already been contacted; what we wanted to do was identify new potential investors. This was a critical decision and it required careful consideration.

In addition to our discussions with the Bank's existing internal staff and external advisors, I suggested that we take a fresh look at the situation and invite a couple of additional people to review our status and alternatives. I wanted to make certain that we not only considered every possible alternative but also sought the widest range of advice possible.

Rusnak agreed, and we made arrangements to meet again with Matt Byrnes from SuNova Capital in New York. Matt had visited Spokane in early 2009 to interview key executives and review the Bank's financial position. I had worked with Byrnes on numerous troubled bank recapitalizations in the early 1990's when we both had a relationship with Keefe Partners, a hedge fund organized by Harry Keefe. Rusnak and I wanted a "fresh independent opinion" of the Bank and our question for Byrnes was simple, "Do you think this Bank can be saved?"

Byrnes has a wealth of experience and I trusted him to be candid in his assessment. Anyone who has worked with Byrnes knows he can analyze data, ask a thousand questions, remember the answers and make a concise and insightful conclusion. His conclusion was again encouraging: "This Bank deserves to be saved."

The second call was to my friend Ed Herlihy, an attorney specializing in financial transactions at Wachtell Lipton in New York. I had worked with Herlihy on several previous banking transactions (including Trans Financial) and always found him to be very insightful. Herlihy was actively involved in negotiations relating to all the major events that had occurred during and in the aftermath of the 2008 financial meltdown. He was well acquainted with all the major players in the bank investment world.

Our experience to date suggested that AmericanWest was just the wrong size to attract more serious investor attention. It was too small for the major investors who wanted to invest $100 million with a maximum position of 24.9% and too large for hedge funds with diversification requirements limiting their investments to $5-$10 million with a 4.9% investment maximum.

The Bank's financial projections now indicated a capital requirement in the $150 million range, and arranging 20+ investors at the same time on the same terms was like "herding cats" under the best of circumstances. Herlihy agreed with our assessment concerning the focus of traditional bank investors.

February 2, 2010: Having discussed the potential alternatives with numerous internal and external advisors, Rusnak and I decided to explore other alternatives to identify new investors and arranged a meeting with Cappello Capital, the boutique investment banking firm in Los Angeles.

The presentation by the Cappello team was very professional and encouraging. The Cappello team indicated they had done significant homework on AmericanWest and the market for bank securities. They were confident that they could identify a lead investor from their client base by the end of March, have an investment group identified by the end of April, a definitive agreement signed by the end of May and be in a position to complete a transaction in July.

This aggressive timeline was an essential part of the decision to retain Cappello Capital as the Company's lead investment banker. The Bank's capital ratios had continued to decline and it was unclear if AmericanWest could avoid seizure past July without the addition of new capital.

February 18, 2010 (AWBC Stock $.47): The Company announced the engagement of Cappello Capital of Santa Monica, California, to serve as financial advisor. The Company's press release stated:

*"We are excited about the prospect of working with Cappello Capital to present AmericanWest's opportunities to potential investors,"* commented Rusnak. *"Cappello Capital is an internationally recognized investment bank with an impressive track record in the arena of private equity investments in public companies, decades of successful transaction experience and a client base spanning the globe. I am looking forward to working with the experienced professionals at Cappello to present AmericanWest's investment thesis to a new investor audience that does not have a government assistance prerequisite. While*

*there can be no assurance of a successful transaction, we are convinced that the combination of the advice and assistance from Cappello Capital with the progress we have made to date with Sandler O'Neill will provide AmericanWest with the best platform for pursuing a successful recapitalization."*

I personally found Glowasky's willingness to accept Cappello Capital as the Company's lead investment banker for the approach to non-traditional bank investors to be incredibly professional. He really did have the best interest of his client at heart.

February 26, 2010: As expected, the Bank received a PCA notice from the FDIC to recapitalize within 30 days or accept an offer to be acquired by another financial institution by March 28, 2010.

Few banks that received a PCA had been able to avoid seizure by bank regulators. In fact, of the 30 banks in the FDIC's Western Region that received a PCA during 2009-10 period, 26 were ultimately seized within an average of 68 days. Time was short; the keys to the Bank were now clearly on the table for the WDFI and FDIC.

The next 90 days were focused on Cappello's efforts to raise capital for AmericanWest. They did successfully identify a potential lead investor; however, the capital commitment was limited to $5 million and required that the investor's firm manage the Bank's non-performing assets after completion of a transaction. This was not as encouraging as we had hoped but negotiations were reported to be occurring with other more substantial investors that could provide a more solid platform.

By May, however, it became clear that the attempt to obtain funding from non-traditional bank investors was not going to produce the required amount of new capital. It was another dead end.

The Bank was past the PCA deadline and was quickly running out of time. Rusnak and I notified Cappello that the Bank needed to change direction and was re-engaging with Glowasky at Sandler O'Neill.

During this period, Rusnak and I continued to discuss alternative structures. It was becoming increasingly clear that assumption or repayment of the $40 million of TruPS at the Company level (nearly $50 million with deferred dividends) was becoming a serious impediment to obtaining new investment at the Company level.

The question of discounting the TruPS position had been raised as early as February 2009 by several experienced investors. However, AmericanWest's TruPS issues were part of several investment pools and it was not possible to identify and negotiate discounts with individual holders of the securities. The key to negotiating a discount was the ability and willingness of the TruPS investment pools' trustee to negotiate.

An encouraging development had taken place in October 2009 when Bimini Capital Management, a real estate investment trust (REIT), had redeemed its outstanding TruPS securities at a substantial discount. It appeared a technique had now been developed that would permit AmericanWest to redeem its outstanding TruPS at a discount.

The good news was premature as litigation was filed against the REIT's trustee on December 23, 2009 to block the Bimini transaction. The net effect of this litigation was an abrupt across the board stop to efforts to redeem TruPS at a discount as no trustee wanted to act until a court issued a final opinion.

At this late stage, Rusnak and I began to seriously discuss recapitalizing the Bank, rather than the holding company. Such a unique strategy would involve issues that to our knowledge had never been tested. If we pursued this alternative it appeared that existing shareholders would receive no consideration, as the TruPS holders would claim any remaining assets at the Company level.

Rusnak made the decision to forge ahead and prepare materials for the Board to consider – every alternative needed to be explored if the Bank was to be saved.

# Chapter Eleven

# Question of Bankruptcy

It was becoming abundantly clear that potential investors were not willing to invest in the Company if it required full recognition of the amount due on the almost $50 million of outstanding TruPS. On the other hand, if recapitalization took place at the Bank level it was obvious the Company would need to declare bankruptcy. This was a daunting thought.

Over the past two years Sandler O'Neill alone had contacted approximately 100 potential investors and executed confidentiality agreements with over 65 so they could conduct due diligence. Glowasky and his team had made a remarkable effort attempting to recapitalize the Company.

June 30, 2010: The Company's financial statements indicated it had only $3.5 million of equity remaining and would soon be insolvent. The recapitalization of the Company had reached an unmistakable dead end. The only remaining hope was a recapitalization at the Bank level.

From the beginning, the Bank's capital restoration plans submitted to bank regulators had contained an option to add capital to the Bank rather than the Company – but the plans had never presented a strategy that required bankruptcy at the holding Company level.

Chartwell prepared a memo for discussion with the Board of Directors that outlined an approach to recapitalize the Bank rather than the Company. This would be a tough alternative for Board members to consider.

Bankruptcy at the holding company level would render the Company's outstanding shares worthless. The latest proxy reported that Board members and executive management owned over 600,000 shares that at $20 per share in late 2007 had represented over $12 million in value. Those shares would now be worthless with no chance of recovery.

As a practical matter, the Company's shares were already essentially worthless with no chance to return to previous levels. The shares were trading at less than a quarter of a dollar, under $0.25, and had been delisted by NASDAQ on March 4, 2010 – shareholder value had declined by over $350 million during the past two years and the total shareholder value was less than $5 million. The value of AWBC shares was already nominal and would be completely worthless if the Bank were to be seized by bank regulators.

Photo: Williams
Jay Simmons, General Counsel

The Board signed on to the bankruptcy strategy after considerable debate and discussion with the Bank's legal and financial advisors. Glowasky had his marching orders and Jay Simmons, AmericanWest's General Counsel, initiated steps to start the process.

Simmons joined Rusnak at AmericanWest in April 2008. Prior to accepting the position at AmericanWest he had been Vice President and Legal Counsel for Zions Bank, a position he had accepted after the acquisition of Trans Financial in Kentucky where he and Rusnak had worked together in the 1990's.

Another encouraging development was the recent organization of several new investment funds to be registered as bank holding companies. These newly organized funds would be in a position to make $100 million plus investments and could be approved by the Federal Reserve for ownership interests as high as 100%. The profile of these new funds now fit the investment requirements of AmericanWest.

Simmons and Rusnak selected Morrison & Foerster (MoFo) in San Francisco and Henry Fields, an attorney at MoFo, as the lead attorney for the proposed transaction. Fields had worked with Rusnak and myself in 2001 to help liquidate the leasing subsidiary at Humboldt Bank. Simmons' initial discussions with Fields, about another possible engagement topic, revealed that MoFo had already thought through the process that AmericanWest was proposing, so AmericanWest engaged MoFo to handle the bankruptcy and regulatory legal work.

Fields and his team immediately engaged with the Bank's regulatory law firm Roberts & Kaplan, and Simmons identified the Foster Pepper firm in Seattle to serve as local bankruptcy counsel for the Company.

Maybe the stars were finally aligning for AmericanWest, but a lot of work needed to be done to structure and negotiate a transaction that had not yet been attempted by a commercial bank.

The final structure took many turns along the way driven by both accounting and legal considerations. Simmons guided the process from a legal viewpoint and he deserves an enormous amount of credit for the successful outcome.

Prior to this time, a bank holding company had only declared bankruptcy "after" the FDIC had seized and sold its banking subsidiary in a "closed bank" transaction. Once its banking subsidiary was seized and sold by the FDIC a holding company had no remaining assets to compensate creditors, such as TruPS, and the holding company was forced to declare bankruptcy.

AmericanWest was proposing to have its holding company declare bankruptcy "before" the Bank would be sold to an investor (not the FDIC) in an "open bank" transaction. The investor would agree to buy the Bank from the holding company during the bankruptcy process. The purchase price for the Bank would be approximately $6 million, $44 million less than the nearly $50 million due on the TruPS debt outstanding at the Company.

The bankruptcy structure needed to find a path that did not require either shareholder approval or approval by the TruPS investors. Neither group was likely to approve a transaction that provided no value to shareholders and a significantly discounted payment to the TruPS investors. MoFo indicated that such a structure was possible with a Chapter 11 bankruptcy filing, under which the Company, as debtor-in-possession, would sell the Bank in Section 363 sale. This would provide for a court approved auction of the Bank with no shareholder or TruPS investor approvals required.

The economics of this potential transaction for new investors were significantly enhanced by a structure that avoided the assumption or repayment of almost $50 million of TruPS related debt.

The bankruptcy strategy moved forward with legal services provided by the MoFo team working closely with Simmons and Rusnak. At this stage, I became largely a spectator watching a first class team execute a very complex plan. The MoFo legal team was confident that a bankruptcy transaction could be completed in a 6-week time frame once an investor was identified and a definitive agreement executed. Bank regulators were somewhat skeptical but indicated they would consider a plan that added the required amount of capital to the Bank.

Plenty of hurdles remained. Potential investors expressed concerns over pursuing this strategy, based on the risk of spending significant time and resources (including the opportunity cost of not pursuing other deals), only to be outbid in the Section 363 auction and losing the Bank to a competing bidder. And potential investors and bank regulators both expressed concerns that any announcement of the bankruptcy of the Company could cause depositors to lose confidence in the Bank and result in significant deposit withdrawals and a "liquidity event" that would force the regulators to seize the Bank. AmericanWest still had to find a willing investor, and deal with regulatory concerns.

Glowasky and his team played the most important role in this effort as they hit the phones again and presented this very unique approach for investor consideration. The response was mixed; many potential investors were very skeptical such a transaction could be completed while others were more optimistic and at least willing to take a look. It is suspected that a few of these potential investors were in reality just curious "tire kickers" but given the structure it took only one, rather than a group of 20 or more, of the new breed of registered bank holding company funds to complete a transaction. The odds had now shifted somewhat in the Bank's favor.

Sandler O'Neill contacted fourteen potential investors during the efforts to remarket the Bank under the newly proposed holding company bankruptcy structure. This included ten new potential investors that executed confidentiality agreements.

In early July the Bank began negotiating an agreement with a potential institutional investor; however, the potential investor could not arrange financing and these negotiations reached another dead end.

SKBHC Holdings LLC (SKBHC) entered the picture in late summer. SKBHC was organized in late 2009 by Scott Kisting and included a Goldman Sachs fund, Oak Tree Capital and several other institutional investors as significant investors.

Prior to organizing SKBHC Kisting was Co-Head of the Global Banking Group for Merrill Lynch Corporation in New York, where he was responsible for $87 billion under management, including personal banking, commercial banking, secured lending, mortgage banking and credit cards. Kisting had over 35 years of banking experience that included executive management roles at California Federal Bank, Norwest Bank and Bank of America.

Experienced bankers, Kisting and his team undertook a very professional approach toward due-diligence and their analysis of the potential investment in the Bank.

SKBHC had already announced the pending acquisition of Starbuck Bancshares, the holding company of The First National Bank of Starbuck, a small $17 million asset bank located in Minnesota. In connection with that transaction, SKBHC had applied to the Federal Reserve for approval to become a registered bank holding company, a process that eventually took eight months. Federal Reserve approval of the Starbuck transaction would be required before AmericanWest could commit to move forward with a transaction with SKBHC.

September 16, 2010: The Bank submitted a combined revised Capital Restoration Plan to the FDIC, WDFI and Federal Reserve that included the proposed bank-level recapitalization plan.

As SKBHC and AmericanWest worked through the process, they met with senior bank regulatory officials to describe the transaction and the process, and to answer questions and address concerns. As they negotiated the terms of the deal, they discussed a communications strategy to limit the risk of customer confusion and significant deposit withdrawals.

AmericanWest had significant experience over the past two years dealing with announcements of negative news, and the Bank's marketing team put together an internal and external communications plan to help reduce the risk of deposit withdrawals. In the end, the Bank's personnel again did an excellent job of managing customer relations and retaining deposit relationships.

October 26, 2010: The Federal Reserve Board announced its approval of the proposal by SKBHC Holdings LLC, Corona del Mar, California, to become a bank holding company and to acquire all the voting shares of Starbuck Bancshares, and indirectly acquire Bancshares' wholly owned subsidiary bank, The First National Bank of Starbuck, both of Starbuck, Minnesota. SKBHC was now in a position to move forward with the AmericanWest transaction.

This announcement allowed the Company to execute the definitive agreement with SKBHC, for the sale of the Bank as part of the Company's soon-to-be-filed Chapter 11 bankruptcy.

October 27, 2010: AmericanWest announced the *agreement to sell and recapitalize its wholly owned subsidiary, AmericanWest Bank which will significantly strengthen the Bank's balance sheet and restore its compliance with regulatory capital requirements.*

SKBHC Holdings LLC, a private investor led by experienced banking professionals, and an affiliated entity (collectively, "SKBHC"), have signed an Asset Purchase Agreement with the Holding Company to acquire all of the common stock of the Bank for a cash payment to the Holding Company of $6.5 million, subject to a competitive bidding process. If SKBHC is the successful bidder, the agreement calls for SKBHC to recapitalize the Bank with additional capital of up to $200 million as required to satisfy the capital requirements imposed by the Bank's federal and state regulators.

To facilitate these transactions, the Holding Company intends to voluntarily file a petition in the U.S. Bankruptcy Court under Chapter 11 of the Bankruptcy Code. Consistent with the Court's procedure under Section 363 of the Code, the Court would supervise a competitive bidding process for the Bank's common stock. Any competing bidder also is expected to be required to recapitalize the Bank to an appropriate level and demonstrate the ability to promptly receive required regulatory approvals.

The Chapter 11 filing would affect only the Holding Company and would exclude its banking subsidiary, AmericanWest Bank and its Far West Bank division, which operate separately from the Holding Company. AmericanWest Bank operates under the name of Far West Bank in Utah.

"This transaction will give AmericanWest Bank and Far West Bank the capital to become 'well-capitalized' and to meet the capital requirements defined by the Bank's regulators – without any financial assistance from the government or taxpayers," said Pat Rusnak, President & CEO of AmericanWest Bancorporation. "We are pleased to have found a partner with extensive banking experience and a strong interest in enabling AmericanWest Bank to grow as a viable competitor that serves thousands of individuals and businesses in our communities."

"Throughout this process, the Bank will continue to provide customers with the same great service they have come to expect," said Rusnak. "Customers will have full access to their accounts and the Bank's other services. Our most recent financial results demonstrate that the Bank has significant liquidity to meet its financial obligations. And customers can rest assured that their deposits continue to be safe, and, as always, are insured to the fullest extent possible by the FDIC."

"This recapitalization of the Bank will satisfy the only significant regulatory requirement that the Bank has not yet achieved through its recovery process. The additional capital will enable us to do even more to meet the needs of our loan customers going forward, and will allow us to return to more normal lending levels after 18 months of dramatically curtailed lending activities due to the constraints that resulted from our lower capital levels," he added.

The Bank maintains strong levels of liquidity to meet its obligations. In another news release issued today, the Holding Company announced that its total balance sheet liquidity as of September 30, 2010 – comprised of cash, cash equivalents and securities – stood at $334 million, up from $233 million on June 30, 2010.

The Bank is regulated separately from the Holding Company, both at the federal and state levels. In compliance with regulatory orders in place since August 2008, the Bank has not paid dividends or transferred funds to the Holding Company since the third quarter of

2008, thus ensuring that the Bank's resources remain at the Bank level.

The Holding Company's Board of Directors has unanimously approved the transaction with SKBHC and the Holding Company intends to petition the Bankruptcy Court to expedite its approval of the proposed sale and recapitalization of the Bank. The Holding Company believes the transaction, which is also subject to regulatory as well as Court approval, will be completed by the end of this year.

"We have been actively engaged over the past two years in seeking additional capital, but no qualified investor has been willing to put new capital into the Holding Company without resolution, such as a discounted settlement, of its existing creditor claims," said Craig D. Eerkes, Chairman of the Board of the Holding Company. "The Court-supervised Chapter 11 process will give the Holding Company an effective way to handle those claims while preserving the value of the Bank's franchise for the community."

The Holding Company does not expect to have sufficient assets to satisfy all of the claims of its creditors. The Holding Company expects that, as a result, creditors will receive less than the value of their claims and that the Holding Company will have no remaining assets to distribute to shareholders.

Scott Kisting, Chairman and Chief Executive Officer of SKBHC, said, "We at SKBHC Holdings LLC believe that community banking has a bright future in the Inland Northwest and Utah. A well-regarded community bank like AmericanWest Bank can play a role in that future. If the court and the regulators approve the proposed transaction, SKBHC will invest up to $200 million of our $750 million in funding commitments, as well as the expertise and dedication of our experienced senior executive team, to recapitalize AmericanWest Bank and position it to grow."

Sandler O'Neill + Partners, L.P. served as the Holding Company's financial advisor, and Morrison & Foerster LLP served as the Holding Company's legal advisor, and the Holding Company intends to apply for both to continue advising the Holding Company on the transaction during the pendency of the bankruptcy proceeding. SKBHC's legal advisor is Skadden, Arps, Slate, Meagher & Flom LLP.

On October 28, 2010, AmericanWest announced that the holding company voluntarily filed a Chapter 11 petition in the U.S. Bankruptcy Court for the Eastern District of Washington.

# # #

AmericanWest had announced but not yet completed the recapitalization of the Bank. It had been over 240 days since the Bank failed to comply with the FDIC's PCA. The average time between the issuance of a PCA and the seizure of others banks was only 68 days. Thanks to strong liquidity and candid regulatory communication, Rusnak had kept his hand on the keys to the Bank an additional 172 days!

Rusnak had been engaged in numerous detailed discussions and meetings with bank regulators during the months preceding the bankruptcy announcement. Regulators were constantly apprised of the Bank's recapitalization efforts and regulators had remained supportive of the Bank's efforts.

The benefits of constant communication and candid assessments were evident. Once SKBHC entered the negotiations, SKBHC was included in exploring the proposed transaction in depth with all the regulatory agencies involved in the process.

Two significant events could disrupt the proposed transaction. The first was legal action by TruPS investors to block the proposed transaction that would significantly discount the value of the AmericanWest TruPS in their respective investment pools. The second would be the entry of additional bidders in the bankruptcy process.

November 18, 2010: As anticipated, Hildene Capital Management, an investor in the TruPS pools that had earlier in the year announced its "pay par or fail" philosophy to discounted tender offers for TruPS, filed a motion with the bankruptcy court to intervene in the court proceedings in regard to its TruPS investment. Eventually, Deutsche Bank and Zions Bancorporation filed motions supporting Hildene's intervention.

The bankruptcy court held a lengthy hearing on November 17 and issued the following ruling:

*THIS MATTER came on for hearing before the Honorable Patricia C. Williams on November 18, 2010 on the Issue of Standing re Deutsche Bank AG, London Branch; Hildene Capital Management, LLC; and Zions Bancorporation. The Court reviewed the files and records herein, heard argument of the parties and was fully advised in the premises. NOW, THEREFORE,*

*IT IS HEREBY ORDERED, ADJUDGED AND DECREED as follows:*

*1. The court's oral ruling constitute the Findings of Fact and Conclusions of Law.*

*2. Deutsche Bank AG, London Branch; Hildene Capital Management, LLC; and Zions Bancorporation do not having standing as parties in interest in these bankruptcy proceedings.*

The court's ruling paved the way for the process to move forward to the next step, the submission of bids to purchase the Bank by any other interested parties. As part of the auction process under Section 363, AmericanWest's attorneys had notified potentially interested parties, including all potential investors who had at any time over the past two years expressed interest in AmericanWest, that they could participate in due diligence and the bidding process. At this point both Columbia Banking System in Tacoma, Washington, and another private equity fund had expressed interest in considering a bid. Both parties were given access to all materials in the Company's virtual data room, and Columbia Banking System conducted several days of on-site due diligence.

November 29, 2010: The deadline for submitting bids had passed and no additional bids were submitted to the bankruptcy court. SKBHC was now in a position to move forward to regulatory approval and the final court hearing to approve the purchase.

December 2, 2010: The Federal Reserve approved the acquisition of AmericanWest Bank by SKBHC Holdings. Another significant step was completed. The FDIC and WDFI followed shortly with their necessary approvals. The Federal Reserve approval required a 15-day waiting period before the sale could be consummated – no earlier than December 17.

December 9, 2010: The bankruptcy court approved the purchase of the Bank by SKBHC from AmericanWest Bancorporation. SKBHC could now move forward with plans to acquire and recapitalize the Bank.

The Bank's operations had made steady progress during the year and would provide a solid platform for future growth.

AmericanWest's asset quality problems had peaked in 2009, and asset quality was now improving. The Bank had recognized loan losses in excess of $150 million since the beginning of 2008. Foreclosed properties had peaked earlier in 2010 at over $55 million and had declined by $10 million during the year. The Bank's Credit Administration and Special Asset groups were successfully resolving problem loans and selling foreclosed properties.

The Bank's liquidity had also continued to improve during 2010 and exceeded $450 million, a $600 million improvement from the summer of 2008!

## AmericanWest Bank: 2010

| $ million | 1Q10 | 2Q10 | 3Q10 | 10/2010 |
|---|---|---|---|---|
| Assets | $1,555 | $1,483 | $1,534 | $1,527 |
| Loans | $1,158 | $1,102 | $1,055 | $1,043 |
| Capital (a) | $ 45 | $ 39 | $ 35 | $ 33 |
| NPA | $ 147 | $ 135 | $ 132 | $ 132 |
| Liquidity (b) | $ 315 | $ 347 | $ 441 | $ 468 |
| Capital % (c) | 2.94 % | 2.64 % | 2.29 % | 2.17 % |

(a) Bank Tangible Capital
(b) Total Liquidity Net of Broker CDs
(c) Tangible Assets divided by Tangible Capital

However, tangible capital at the Bank level was now quickly approaching the threshold for the Bank to be seized. The keys to the Bank were not only on the table but were within reach of the WDFI and FDIC.

The saving of AmericanWest Bank had come down to the wire – no time to spare!

My frustrations concerning unclear or inconsistent bank regulatory policy have been expressed throughout the preceding chapters and my views are covered in more detail in the final chapter.

However, it is very important to recognize that every bank regulatory agency involved in the successful completion of AmericanWest's unique recapitalization proposal was exceptionally cooperative and supportive as the plan was negotiated, announced and progressed through the bankruptcy court.

No regulatory roadmap existed to guide the bankruptcy process and approval required thoughtful consideration – bank regulators were all sailing into uncharted waters. The Federal Reserve, the FDIC and the WDFI are all to be complimented for their thoughtful consideration of a unique plan, avoiding bureaucratic delays and approving each step in a timely manner.

The legal and regulatory process had moved forward as predicted by the legal team at MoFo, final bankruptcy court approval of the transaction had been granted six weeks after the initial announcement – just like clockwork.

December 16, 2010: The officers and employees of AmericanWest arranged a surprise "Thank You" tribute for Rusnak at the Support Center with conference call links to every office. For Simmons and myself this tribute was somewhat bittersweet, as we already knew Rusnak's "transition days" were numbered.

Rusnak was presented with an a heartfelt, leather bound "In Gratitude" book consisting of family photographs and personal "thank you" messages from the employees at every bank location for his dedication and leadership.

Rusnak was also presented with an electric guitar to replace one he lost in a fire as a token of appreciation for a job well done.

I was grateful to be included - words cannot describe the emotion and appreciation displayed by all in attendance at that "Thank You" tribute.

Photo: McPhee

The plaque inside the case was inscribed:

***Patrick J Rusnak, President & CEO***
***AmericanWest & Far West Bank***
***In Gratitude for Your Rock Star Performance***
***Your Senior Management Team, December 2010***

December 17, 2010: On Friday I headed to the Spokane airport, participated in a final Board conference call and boarded my flight back to Florida. My assignment was now complete.

December 20, 2010: On Monday the transaction was completed with SKBHC's purchase of AmericanWest Bank from the AmericanWest Bancorporation for $6.5 million and the investment by SKBHC of $185 million into AmericanWest Bank. SKBHC became the new owner of AmericanWest Bank.

SKBHC's management team included individuals that were to be named to the top three executive positions of any SKBHC acquisition. As a result, Rusnak officially introduced the new executive team from SKBHC to the Bank's employees.

Scott Kisting was introduced as the Bank's new President & CEO, James Claffee became the new Chief Operating Officer and Peter Conner the new Chief Financial Officer. The new executive team from SKBHC now filled each of the positions that had been held by Rusnak for the past two and one-half years. In addition, SKBHC, as the Bank's new shareholder, elected a new Board of Directors.

December 20$^{th}$ marked the beginning of a new chapter for AmericanWest Bank as a "well-capitalized" financially strong institution. The Board and Rusnak had achieved their final goal of saving the Bank from seizure by the FDIC and protecting the jobs of over 500 employees at AmericanWest.

Rusnak handed the keys to the Bank to the new executive management team - he then drove home to enjoy the Christmas holidays with his family.

# Chapter Twelve

## Tone at the Top

What separated AmericanWest Bank from the more than 300 banks that have failed in the past three years?

Leadership at every level made a difference. So a few observations on the Bank's leadership in general and Rusnak's leadership style seem appropriate.

The "Tone at the Top" was visible and consistent. Rusnak's approach to dealing with problems was contagious; accept the facts ("It Is What It Is"), don't wallow in denial, don't waste time with the "blame game", identify and implement a solution.

Decisions were made - not deferred or avoided. Once the facts were clear decisions were made, implemented and supported. Management changes, closing branch offices, staff reductions, problem loan recognition, foreclosed property sales and other tough decisions were made promptly and communicated. This was true at all levels; the Board, executive management and operating management. Bank employees got the message – authority to make operating decisions was delegated down to the appropriate level - not delegated up to the CEO or the Board.

Rusnak led by example – he was visible to other employees throughout the Bank and no doubt word traveled that he worked as hard and as long (from his small office at the Support Center) as anybody in the organization. Frequent all-employee conference calls with the CEO that included open questions and candid answers kept employees informed and engaged.

The Board and Rusnak always kept an "open mind" and sought the best advice available. Rusnak didn't try to impress others with how much he knew; he asked questions and wanted to learn what others knew about a topic. He constantly spoke with a wide variety of people (bankers, attorneys, accountants, investment bankers, consultants and bank regulators) and consistently asked questions to learn more about the topic at hand.

The Bank avoided corporate "perks" in an age of sacrifice. The Bank had no company aircraft and Rusnak drove his own pickup truck, not a company owned luxury car. He didn't even have a reserved parking space. The negative reaction I have witnessed at other banks when tone-deaf corporate executives arrive in the company plane or company owned Cadillac to announce expense cuts and employee layoffs did not occur at AmericanWest.

Past experience and mentors obviously played an important role. The Bank was fortunate to have the right person in the right place at a critical time. I have no doubt that seeing the example set by Berta in Kentucky helped build a foundation for Rusnak's development. Berta was a beneficiary of his past relationship with Grissom at Citizens Fidelity (as was I). Mentors make a difference and many people at AmericanWest will benefit in the future from their experience with Rusnak.

Qualified bankers are in short supply. I was very impressed throughout the past three years that Rusnak and his management team were not only able to retain talented employees but also attract talented people. Even in the toughest of times Rusnak kept a "can do" constructive attitude – "Tone at the Top" makes a significant difference.

# Chapter Thirteen

# Regulatory Policy

One benefit of being the author of this book is the opportunity to write from my own perspective and to insert my own opinions throughout the text. This final chapter will address a few of the policy issues that I believe contributed to the financial meltdown that occurred in 2008-09.

As indicated throughout the book, government and regulatory policies frequently create considerable frustration for me. However, it's very important to make a clear distinction between regulatory policy and the people working at regulatory agencies.

During the past several years I have spoken at numerous banking conferences across the country and this chapter reflects the issues I have addressed in many of those presentations.

As always, a disclaimer is in order: these views on regulatory policy are mine and mine alone, not the views of AmericanWest, its Board of Directors or management.

# # #

Bank regulators have a thankless job. They have no career upside if they even attempt to do something that might be viewed as helping the industry and they are subject to severe criticism if anything goes wrong. Watching any Congressional hearing on TV clearly illustrates the toxic "blame game" in which they are expected to regulate our financial services industry. It must be tempting to regulate in anticipation of an Inspector General's final report, not for the good of the banking system or any individual bank.

Regulators stationed outside of Washington D.C. are expected to carry out policy, not make policy, so they have little if any flexibility. My experience with bank regulators across the country has always been very positive – they are quality people attempting to do a professional job under very stressful circumstances. I have however experienced frustrating inconsistencies in the application of regulatory policy across the country. However, I attribute this primarily to a lack of clear policy direction from Washington D.C.

Media reports based on interviews with selected bank executives often refer to cases of unnecessary loan write-downs and heavy-handed actions by regulators. Frankly, in the cases where Chartwell has played a role in such situations we have found regulatory action to be generally appropriate. As events unfolded in the current financial crisis, some bankers were simply caught as the "deer in the (economic) headlights."

It is essential for directors and bank executives at any troubled institution to build a professional and candid relationship with their regulators. Rusnak not only understood this, but also did the best job of frequent and consistent communication with all the Bank's regulators that I have witnessed. Rusnak's practice of conveying "It Is What It Is" and the facts were communicated without any political "spin."

Having made the distinction between people and policy I will now share a few of my thoughts on the unintended consequences of regulatory policy.

### Bank Policy: Management Approvals

As I have already discussed in Chapter Five the time required for bank regulators to approve the promotion of an existing executive to a new position – especially when that individual is to be the interim CEO – creates unnecessary uncertainty.

Bank boards and management are expected to implement "prompt corrective action" without receiving prompt regulatory approval of their selection of new executive management. This requirement also makes it very difficult for bank boards to recruit new qualified executives who are currently employed, as those executives are being asked to risk submitting their resignation before they obtain regulatory approval for their new executive position.

### Bank Policy: Executive Compensation

The requirement to obtain regulatory approval for the payment of any funds that bank regulators may deem to be severance creates a significant dilemma for bank boards. Troubled banks need to downsize operations, and that includes the need to downsize people – some jobs for good people simply need to disappear. In my experience, such payments are seldom if ever authorized by bank regulators and this policy is very unfair in many circumstances.

In other cases, nonpayment may just set up a legal dispute with terminated executives who may have contractual rights, and create an expensive legal distraction for the bank. I concur that executives who were part of the problem should not receive severance – but labor law and the courts may not always agree.

The Dodd-Frank Act includes provisions that address board and regulatory oversight of executive officer pay and incentive compensation. I suspect the Dodd-Frank Act may impact board compensation committees in a way that's similar to the impact Sarbanes-Oxley had on bank audit committees.

### Bank Policy: Capital Ratios

Regulatory policy concerning appropriate "risk adjusted" capital ratios was introduced without publication, discussion or notification as the 2008-09 bank capital crisis unfolded. "Well capitalized" banks were required to add capital. Published Consent Orders, that required capital ratios that were substantially above those required by FDICIA, became a proxy for the new regulatory policy.

Many community banks were required to increase capital ratios above "well capitalized" levels at a time when capital markets were closed. The only alternative open to them to increase capital ratios was to downsize their balance sheet by reducing the size of the loan portfolio.

The math is rather simple: when the market for new capital is closed, any regulatory requirement to increase minimum capital ratios by 1% creates the unintended consequence of reducing assets (loans) by 10%. Banks across the country didn't know what bank regulators might require as a result of the bank's next exam. Even good banks were reducing loans at the very time elected officials were asking banks to make more loans to support the economy.

The Dodd-Frank Act also makes reference to a requirement for a capital "cushion", a concept that adds more uncertainty to potential regulatory requirements.

### Bank Policy: Hedge Funds

The requirement for banks owned by institutional investors (such as hedge funds) to maintain capital ratios higher than those required of other bank holding companies is counterproductive to the regulatory goal of adding new capital to the banking system.

Investors in any capitalistic system expect to earn a competitive rate of return. Setting higher capital standards that reduce investment returns is not the way for bank regulators to attract new capital.

## U.S. Treasury: TARP & CPP

TARP was introduced as an unworkable program to purchase troubled assets from banks, but fortunately it was quickly converted into a program to add capital to the banking system when none was available from the capital markets. The delay in defining the rules, the uncertainty surrounding who qualified, and bad publicity related to its use for supporting AIG and other troubled institutions (including the auto companies) all damaged the reputation of the program.

However, when the CPP program was expanded to include community banks it did provide a unique opportunity for many community banks to obtain capital "insurance" in a very uncertain economic climate.

## FDIC: Liquidity & Brokered CDs

The unintended consequences created by the failure of the FDIC to approve the issuance of brokered CDs by "adequately capitalized" banks to replace maturing brokered CDs was one of the most disruptive policy decisions made during the past several years.

The banking system was experiencing a serious liquidity challenge and this FDIC policy contributed to the problem, not towards a solution. This issue is further described in Chapter Five.

## FDIC: Deposit Insurance Fund

Media coverage consistently and incorrectly refers to the "Cost to the Taxpayer" when a bank fails. The FDIC Insurance Fund is a "self insurance" fund for the banking system supported by the premiums paid by banks. The FDIC is a government agency funded by the banking system – not by the taxpayer.

Funding policy for the FDIC Insurance Fund was counter-cyclical. No premiums were required when times were good and premiums were increased when credit problems were encountered. The banking system was required to pay more into the FDIC Insurance Fund when it could least afford to do so.

To compound the problem, troubled banks pay a risk-adjusted premium. Higher premiums for a troubled bank just reduce capital and increase the risk of failure.

I doubt Dodd-Frank solves this problem.

### FDIC: Deposit Insurance

The FDIC did this one right. Increasing the level of deposit insurance coverage was a significant step in helping restore confidence and in protecting liquidity for all banks.

### FASB: Fair Value Accounting

The person who coined the name "Fair Value" for this accounting concept should get a "gold star" from his/her colleagues. It simply sounds un-American to argue against fair value – rather like disparaging the value of motherhood or apple pie. To their credit, bank regulators have voiced concern about the potential negative impact of fair value accounting for many years.

The introduction by FASB of expanded fair value concepts during the early days of the financial crisis was a significant contributor to the uncertainty that disrupted the financial markets. The precision of mathematical models to determine the market value of financial instruments that have no active market is questionable at best.

Fair value plays an important role for entities such as mutual funds or hedge funds that redeem investor funds from the fund itself. On the other hand, fair value has no place in the income statement of banks whose shares are traded between investors, not redeemed by the institution. This fundamental difference seems lost on the proponents of fair value.

Sufficient space is not available to discuss the many flaws of fair value accounting. However, if today's fair value accounting standards had been in place during the 20% interest rate environment of the early 1980's the asset write-downs due only to high interest rates would have resulted in the failure of nearly every bank in the nation. I fail to see how that outcome would have been in the best interest of investors or the citizens of our country.

### FASB: Purchase Accounting

The FASB eliminated pooling accounting in June 2001 for all mergers; all future transactions were to be subject to purchase accounting treatment. I am not going to pass judgment on the technical merits of pooling versus purchase accounting - there were good arguments on both sides of the question.

However, an analysis of FDIC data indicates that purchase accounting added over $16 billion of goodwill to the financial statements of smaller regional and community banks ($1 to $10 billion asset size) over the nine years preceding the 2008-09 financial crisis. Goodwill impairment charges during 2008-10 have reduced that amount by $10 billion (over $100 million in 2008 at AmericanWest). Goodwill would not have been recorded if these acquisitions had been completed with pooling accounting rather than purchase accounting treatment and such impairment charges would not have been recorded during 2008-10.

Furthermore, pooling required that acquirors could only issue common stock - no new debt could be issued to pay for a pooling transaction. An analysis completed by Chartwell indicated that, in the eight years preceding the 2008-09 financial crisis, smaller regional and community banks had issued $50 billion of TruPS, mostly through TruPS investment pools, to acquire other banks and repurchase stock. This increase in holding company debt (e.g., $40 million of TruPS at

AmericanWest) became a significant hurdle to many potential bank holding company recapitalizations.

The Dodd-Frank Act now limits the use of TruPS as bank capital.

### SEC: Bank Loan Loss Reserves

In 1999 the SEC accused SunTrust Bank of understating reported earnings by increasing the amount the bank allocated to their loan loss reserve. It should be noted the amount of the loan loss reserve is fully disclosed, it's certainly not a secret fund. SunTrust was forced to restate earnings as a result of the SEC's action and all banks were then forced to adopt loan loss reserve formulas based on historical experience.

With a good economy and a few years of minimal loan losses these historical formulas dictated low loan loss reserves. As a consequence, bank loan loss reserves were inadequate to absorb the increase in loan losses as the economy entered the recession of 2008-09.

The SEC's ill-advised action produced a rigid backward looking formula that assumed the good times would last forever and prohibited the banking system from being prepared for the 2008-09 downturn in the business cycle.

### SEC: Net Capital Policy

**This is the big one nobody discusses!**

*April 28, 2004: SEC Votes New Net-Capital Rules*

*EXCERPT, SEC Press Release: In a move in line with bank regulatory changes in Europe, the U.S. Securities and Exchange Commission voted unanimously in an open meeting to approve new net-capital rules.*

*Goldman Sachs, Morgan Stanley, Merrill Lynch, Lehman Brothers and Bear Stearns are expected to apply soon to be designated as "consolidated supervised entities," or CSEs.*

*SEC Market Regulation Director Annette Nazareth told reporters after the meeting, "They are all very well-capitalized firms". In line with new capital adequacy standards coming into force soon under Europe's Basel accords, brokerages granted CSE status would be able to use in-house, risk-measuring computer models to figure how much net capital they need to set aside. Under Basel standards, some institutions could soon be cutting their net capital by as much as 50 percent.*

*SEC Commissioner Paul Atkins said monitoring the sophisticated models used by the brokerages under the CSE rules and stepping in where net capital falls too low "is going to present a real management challenge" for the SEC.*

*Since the new CSE rules will apply to the largest brokerages without bank affiliates, SEC Commissioner Harvey Goldschmid said, "If anything goes wrong, it's going to be an awfully big mess."*

An "awfully big mess" was an understatement! This capital policy change by the SEC in 2004 is what permitted the large investment banking firms to increase leverage from a maximum of 20x (5% capital) to over 40x (less than 2.5 %).

In volatile times, such as today, markets frequently move between 1% and 2% a day – enough to wipe out a firm's entire capital account in a couple of days.

Basing the new Basel capital standards on in-house risk-measuring computer models was a policy blunder on a global scale that significantly magnified the liquidity and capital crisis of 2008 – just a few years later.

## Congress: Housing Policy

Home ownership has been a key element of government policy for decades; "everyone should have the opportunity to buy his or her own home" has been a universal political philosophy. Over the years multiple government programs at the federal, state and local government levels have been introduced to help people purchase their own homes, even if they could not afford to make a down payment. A whole new language developed: Option ARM, sub-prime, soft seconds, 120 loans, stated income loans, etc.

Freddie Mac and Fannie Mae, the two housing GSEs that failed in September 2008, became private market tools for government policy. Today they represent a $5 trillion taxpayer burden - the "elephant in the room" that has yet to be addressed by Congress.

The September 2008 financial meltdown can be traced to many factors, including Wall Street greed, but government housing policy provided the fuel for the sub-prime mortgage explosion and subsequent implosion.

Community banks largely avoided such sub-prime lending products; AmericanWest did virtually no sub-prime mortgage lending. However, when the mortgage music stopped on Wall Street, potential house buyers could not obtain a mortgage; home sales came to a halt; developers could not sell the lots they had developed; local builders could not sell the houses and condos they had built that had been financed by regional/community banks; companies that supplied labor and materials to the housing industry suffered; and the local banks faced an increasing level of problem loans. The mortgage crisis on Wall Street moved to Main Street.

## The Dodd–Frank Act

Signed into law July 2010, the Dodd-Frank Act is intended to prevent another financial crisis. It includes 2,300 pages and 1,400 sections, requires 350+ new rules and establishes 7 new departments or agencies. Only time will tell the total (positive and negative) impact the Act will actually have on the banking system.

# # #

I believe these regulatory and government policies were contributing factors to the 2008-09 financial crisis; their combined impact turned what should have been a modest correction into a global liquidity, credit and capital catastrophe.

On the other hand, many individual bankers, bank boards and bank regulators have responded to a very difficult environment in a very positive manner. I remain confident that the financial system will once again provide the financial fuel that is necessary for economic growth.

The AmericanWest story is an outstanding example of perseverance and ingenuity – well done to the Board of Directors, management and all the employees of AmericanWest Bank.

*Charles J Thayer*
Chartwell Capital Ltd
December 2010

# AmericanWest

## Board of Directors

| | |
|---|---|
| | **Craig D. Eerkes**<br>Chairman of the Board<br>AmericanWest Bancorporation<br>AmericanWest Bank<br>President, Sun Pacific Energy, Inc. |
| | **J. Frank Armijo**<br><br>Program Director and General Manager<br>West Coast Programs<br>Lockheed Martin |
| | **Kay C. Carnes**<br><br>Associate Dean<br>Gonzaga University<br>School of Business |
| | **Patrick J. Rusnak**<br><br>President & CEO<br>AmericanWest Bancorporation<br>AmericanWest Bank |
| | **Donald H. Swartz II**<br><br>President<br>J&M Electric |
| | **P. Mike Taylor**<br><br>Director of Engineering Services<br>City of Spokane |

Photos: AmericanWest

# *AmericanWest*
# *Senior Management Team*

| | |
|---|---|
| | **Patrick J. Rusnak**<br>President & CEO<br>AmericanWest Bancorporation<br>AmericanWest Bank |
| | **Wade A. Griffith**<br><br>Executive Vice President<br>Chief Information Officer |
| | **Robert A. Harris**<br>Executive Vice President<br>Chief Banking Officer<br>Washington & Idaho |
| | **Joseph Marchese**<br>Executive Vice President<br>Chief Credit Officer |
| | **B. Nicole Sherman**<br><br>Executive Vice President<br>Chief Banking Officer, Utah |
| | **Jay B. Simmons**<br>Executive Vice President<br>General Counsel |

Photos: AmericanWest

# *AmericanWest*

# *Asset/Liability Committee*

*Members:*

| | |
|---|---|
| Robert Harris | Chief Banking Officer |
| Joseph Marchese | Chief Credit Officer |
| Patrick Rusnak | Chief Executive Officer |
| Nicole Sherman | Chief Banking Officer |
| Jay Simmons | General Counsel |
| Donald Swartz | Board Member |
| Linda Williams | Treasurer, Committee Chair |

*Ex-Officio Members:*

| | |
|---|---|
| Ron Barkley | Senior Credit Administrator |
| Heidi Cleveland | Marketing Director |
| Anthony Gould | Consultant |
| Wade Griffith | Chief Information Officer |
| Jason Hester | Director of Operations |
| Jason King | Financial Analyst |
| Mike Koch | Credit Support Services |
| Shelly Krasselt | Controller |
| Joshua Combs | Financial Analyst |
| Charles Thayer | Financial Advisor |

# The Attorneys

**AmericanWest Bank**

    Jay B Simmons, General Counsel

    Craig M Moore, Associate Counsel

**Foster Pepper PLLP**

    Christopher M Alston, Member

    Dillon E Jackson, Member

**Morrison & Foerster LLP**

    Larry Engel, Partner

    Henry M Fields, Partner

    Kenneth E Kohler, Partner

    Alexandria Steinberg Barrage, Of Counsel

    Jonathan T Keen, Associate

    Dina Kushner, Associate

    Vincent J Novak, Associate

**Roberts Kaplan LLP**

    Andrew H Ognall, Partner

    Kenneth E Roberts, Partner

# *The Author*

Charles J Thayer is Chairman and Managing Director of Chartwell Capital Ltd., a private investment firm providing specialized advisory services to the board of directors and executive management of banks, corporations and institutional investors.

Thayer had a twenty-year career in commercial banking prior to organizing Chartwell Capital in 1990. As Executive Vice President of PNC Financial, Pittsburgh, he had management responsibility for finance, merger and acquisitions, investor relations, strategic planning, and he served as Chairman of PNC Securities Corp, PNC's capital markets subsidiary.

Prior to its acquisition by PNC in 1986, Thayer served as Executive Vice President and Chief Financial Officer of Citizens Fidelity Corporation, Kentucky's largest bank holding company.

He served as an advisor to Keefe Partners LP, New York, from 1990 until 2002. Keefe Partners was a hedge fund founded by Harry V. Keefe (1922-2002) to invest in financial securities.
☐
Thayer was named Chairman of the American Association of Bank Directors in 2007. The AABD is the national non-profit organization dedicated to serving the information, education and advocacy needs of financial institution directors.

Thayer's board positions currently include the Cystic Fibrosis Foundation, Washington, DC; Louisville Community Bancorp and National Association of Corporate Directors (Florida).

He previously served on the boards of Sunbeam Corporation, where he served as interim Chairman & CEO in 1993; CogenAmerica, an independent power producer; Republic Bank - Florida (acquired by BB&T) and BB&T Bank (Florida).

## Abbreviations & Definitions

| | |
|---|---|
| ALCO | Asset/Liability Committee |
| AWBC | Stock symbol for AmericanWest |
| CDs | Bank certificate of deposit |
| | |
| CEO | Chief Executive Officer |
| CFO | Chief Financial Officer |
| COO | Chief Operating Officer |
| | |
| CPP | TARP – Capital Purchase Program |
| CRP | Capital Restoration Plan |
| EVP | Executive Vice President |
| | |
| FDIC | Federal Deposit Insurance Corporation |
| FDICIA | FDIC Improvement Act of 1991 |
| FED | Federal Reserve Bank |
| | |
| FHFA | Federal Housing Finance Agency |
| FHLB | Federal Home Loan Bank |
| GSE | Government Sponsored Agency |
| | |
| MBA | Masters of Business Administration |
| NASDAQ | National Stock Exchange |
| NPA | Non Performing Asset |
| | |
| OREO | Other Real Estate Owned (Foreclosed) |
| PCA | Prompt Corrective Action |
| REIT | Real Estate Investment Trust |
| | |
| SAD | Special Assets Division |
| SEC | Securities & Exchange Commission |
| SVP | Senior Vice President |
| | |
| TARP | Troubled Asset Relief Program |
| TruPS | Trust Preferred Securities |
| WDFI | Washington Dept of Financial Institutions |

## Tombstone

**$600 MILLION**
NET LIQUIDITY IMPROVEMENT
AmericanWest ALCO Team
JULY 2008 – DECEMBER 2010

**$185 MILLION**
SKBHC HOLDINGS LLC
CAPITAL INVESTMENT
DECEMBER 2010

---

The undersigned served as a financial advisor to

**AmericanWest Bancorporation**
and
**AmericanWest Bank**

## CHARTWELL CAPITAL LTD

Made in the USA
Lexington, KY
26 February 2011